The Articulate Advocate

New Techniques of Persuasion for Trial Lawyers

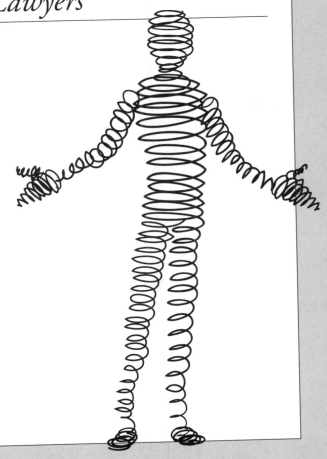

The Articulate Advocate is a must read for anyone who must speak well before audiences big or small. For lawyers in court, before the media, or in the boardroom, it is close to malpractice not to read and practice its wisdom.

—Paul J. Zwier, Professor of Law, Emory University, Atlanta, GA

Following the practical advice in *The Articulate Advocate* is proof positive that we all can get better at what we do. A must read for anyone who makes a living in a courtroom, [it] belongs on the bookshelf of every trial lawyer, young, old, and in between.

—William Jack, Smith Haughey Rice & Roegge, Grand Rapids, MI

...a brilliant little book that I highly recommend.... *The Articulate Advocate* teaches you everything you ever wanted to know about oral advocacy, but didn't know how – or whom – to ask. Providing more than a powerful toolkit, Johnson and Hunter convey, in simple language and easily appreciated metaphors, just enough of the science for you to understand how to skillfully use your body's hardwiring and your brain's operating system to maximum advantage.

—Michael Halberstam, Junior Fellow at the Center for Law and Economic Studies, Columbia Law School, New York, NY

Johnson and Hunter's insights in this book are better than Prozac and Valium for the nervous litigator.

—Honorable Nancy Vaidik, State Court of Appeals, Indianapolis, IN

[An] indispensable guide to effective courtroom communication....Johnson and Hunter give the trial lawyer an array of strategies...to overcome "public speaking anxiety" and to act naturally in a highly stressful and artificial situation.

—Professor James Carey, School of Law, Loyola University Chicago, IL

...A succinct and clearly written guide that will help every courtroom lawyer get more comfortable thinking on their feet while they speak—and speaking on their feet while they think.

—Steven D. McCormick, Kirkland & Ellis, Chicago, IL

The Articulate Advocate is essential reading for anyone who wants to try cases. No matter how many trials you may have under your belt, you'll find many useful and original insights on how to communicate with juries and judges, or simply with other human beings. It is well organized, engaging, and easy to read. I unequivocally and wholeheartedly encourage you to consume it from cover to cover.

—Carol B. Anderson, Director of Trial Advocacy, Wake Forest University School of Law, Winston-Salem, NC

[A] manual such as *The Articulate Advocate* is long overdue. It is highly original, clearly written, and extremely helpful.... I have no doubt that this book will be an invaluable guide to young aspiring advocates and to those more experienced hands who are never afraid to keep learning.

—Professor Peter Lyons, CPD Training, York, England

The Articulate Advocate captures all of the helpful tips, insightful analogies, and useful drills that improve your technique in communicating with fact finders. You can't help but be a more persuasive advocate if you take to heart and put it into practice.

—Frank Rothschild, former Judge and Prosecutor, Kilauea, HI

A generation of trial lawyers and teachers of trial advocacy have waited for this book. Here it is: wisdom of thought and instruction for how to say and be a trial lawyer. But more, it is for anyone who would speak for others.

—Thomas H. Singer, Adjunct Professor of Law, University of Notre Dame Law School, South Bend, IN

The Articulate Advocate, like [Johnson and Hunter's] lectures, represents the quintessential work on presentation skills.

—Robert Stein, Robert Stein and Associates, Concord, NH

The
Articulate
Advocate

*New Techniques of Persuasion
for Trial Lawyers*

Brian K. Johnson and Marsha Hunter

CROWN KING BOOKS

Printed in the United States of America on acid-free paper.

Last digit in print number: 0 9 2 0 1 3 5 4 3 2 3

    Johnson, Brian K.
      The articulate advocate : new techniques of
    persuasion for trial lawyers / Brian K. Johnson & Marsha
    Hunter.
      p. cm.
    Includes bibliographical references and index.
    LCCN 2008927449
    ISBN-13: 978-0-9796895-0-5
    ISBN-10: 0-9796895-0-3

      1. Trial practice--United States. 2. Public
    speaking. 3. Communication in law. 4. Persuasion
    (Psychology)   I. Hunter, Marsha. II. Title.

    KF8915.J64 2009   347.73'75
                     QBI08-600351

Cover and book design by Charles Kreloff.
Illustrations by James Kacherlies and Jeanne K. Blahut.

Crown King Books
600 North Fourth Street
Phoenix, Arizona 85004
www.crownkingbooks.com

The right word may be effective,
but no word was ever as effective
as a rightly timed pause.

Mark Twain

Contents

CHAPTER TWO
Your Brain

Chapter Three

Your Voice

CHAPTER FOUR

How to Practice 135

To my parents, Peggy and Eddie,
and my brother Bruce,
my first and most devoted audience.

This book is the life-long synthesis of the wisdom bestowed upon me
by the following mentors. I share with others what each of them taught
me every day that I teach:

I thank Edwin G. Amundson, my first voice teacher, for a love of
performance and the power of projection; Dr. Kenneth Jennings for
the spiritual transcendence of precision through practice; Dr. Robert
Moulton for the grammar and eloquence of body language; Dr. Vern
Sutton for his alchemy of artistry and improvisation; Patricia L. Feld
for pointing my life in this direction and guiding me still; and Prof.
Laurence M. Rose for his early and unflagging loyalty to the evolu-
tion of my ideas. Thanks to my co-author as well. Dr. H. Wesley Balk,
whose techniques are the foundation for everything I teach, constantly
challenged his students with the question, "Is there a better way to say
that?" As a lecturer and communication coach, I still grapple with his
question each day, and I hope this book meets his challenge.

Brian K. Johnson

For Rian and Matt.

Flying an airplane may seem far removed from trial advocacy, but aviation has revealed insights into many of the concepts Brian Johnson and I teach. From my first flying lesson I was intrigued by the sciences that explore human performance and the brain. As I shared tales of my studies with Brian, we began to see the connection between how pilots and lawyers think. I am grateful to my flight instructors, particularly Bruce Jaeger and Brian Addis, for teaching me that thinking on your seat is not much different from thinking on your feet.

Gratitude often springs from surprising juxtapositions. Two disparate parts of my life inspired me as I worked on this book. First, I have a vast collection of mental images of my trial skills students refining their technique. The exciting moment when a witness answers, prompted by the "give" gesture. The light bulb going on when a deep breath throws a formerly timid voice across a large room. The applause from the class when a lawyer catches himself before saying, "And, okay...." The video from a state supreme court appeal, in which my student used a parachute line before pausing to look at her notes, buying herself a moment as she said, "Now, I'd like to get this just right...." The skeptics also were sitting on my shoulder, those who make me explain it again patiently, differently, better.

Always on my mind, also, were the days and nights I spent on stage, first as a professional opera singer, and later as an actor. Gifted colleagues taught me to keep striving for authenticity even while singing unnaturally loudly in giant theaters. Trial work is no less an all-consuming, excessive, and exhilarating profession. And as much as I yearned to be a major star on glamorous stages, I learned more lessons from the high school students on the Navajo Reservation in Many Farms, Arizona, who loved *Don Pasquale*; the middle school students in San Francisco who shushed rowdy hecklers during a love duet; and the 13 senior citizens from North Dakota who came to listen to Stephen Sondheim songs on a blustery April day. All of them showed me that real connection happens when you trust your audience. Audiences, like fact finders, are looking for the truth.

Many people helped me in all the ways authors need nurturing. Mary Lou Humphrey was an indispensable editor and colleague. My parents, Mike and Wen Hunter, were a reliable and constant stream of encouragement and praise. Jeanne Blahut urged courage and lent unflagging support. Jay Leach and Cary Bricker's wonderful teaching notes are available as a free download on the Crown King Books web site. Our NITA colleagues, too many to mention, smiled patiently as we reported, year after year, that this book was making progress. Many colleagues read the book, and their comments made it better. I am grateful to them, too, for being role models for so many of my students.

Marsha Hunter

Introduction

There are so many ways to persuade juries. One trial lawyer has a personal style full of folksy charm, while another argues issues with the tenacity of a pit bull. One lawyer strides dynamically throughout the courtroom, yet another stands absolutely still. One fills the courtroom with a booming voice, while another proves that *less is more* and speaks to the jury in more measured tones. One gestures frequently, another only for emphasis. One goes for the jugular on cross-examination, while another courteously destroys the credibility of the opposing witness and kills with kindness. All of these styles are effective. What an advocate needs to develop, therefore, is a distinctly individual, persuasive style.

Above all, an advocate's style must be personal. You cannot simply mimic what works for your colleagues or your mentor or your opponents, although these role models may be inspiring. Your personal style is a unique combination of elements involving the control and coordination of your body, your brain, and your voice. To discover—or polish, if you are well along in your career—your identity as an articulate advocate, you must experiment with all the varied stylistic elements of courtroom presentation and find those that suit you. Because no single choice works all the time, or under all circumstances, your style ultimately will consist of many diverse elements reconfigured and adapted to meet each advocacy challenge appropriately. In fact, all of the stylistic elements listed in the previous paragraph might describe a single advocate at different phases of trial.

Persuasive style is not based on pretending, acting, or faking it; you must look, sound, and feel authentic to be believable. It may seem logical simply to tell yourself to "be natural" or "be yourself," but that is only part of the solution—for the challenge of being natural is complicated by a surprising paradox.

The Paradox of Naturalness

The word "natural" has many definitions: here it refers to the way you speak, think, and behave regularly and consistently in the course of daily life. If you do something often, it's natural; if you don't, it's not. Paradoxically, some of these *natural* behaviors will make you look and feel *unnatural* in court. And as an advocate you need to consciously employ certain *unnatural* behaviors to look and feel *natural*. What a paradox! To complicate the issue, most people are not aware of their natural behaviors because of this pair of opposites in human behavior: When you are *natural* you are not *self-conscious*. When you are *self-conscious*, you don't feel *natural*. Therefore, you can't just tell yourself to "be natural" in court, because it is unlikely you are fully *conscious* of what your *natural* behavior is. What you need is technique.

Your Body

Consider some of the physical behaviors you display while engaged in everyday conversation. As you speak with a colleague, you unconsciously exhibit certain mannerisms. Perhaps you push your eyeglasses up on your nose, or brush your hair from your face. You may jingle the change in your pocket, fiddle with a pen, or shift your weight back and forth from one leg to the other. Neither you nor your colleague is likely to be aware of, or distracted by, these behaviors. They are normal, unconscious, and natural.

Now imagine that you're standing up in court to address the jury. You tell yourself to be natural, and your body follows that instruction exactly. The jury watches you shift your weight back and forth, push your glasses up on your nose, brush your hair from your brow, fiddle with your pen, and jingle the change in your pocket. Do these behaviors make you look "natural" to that jury? No, far from it.

Under the intense scrutiny of the courtroom, the paradox of naturalness emerges and causes your perfectly normal behaviors to look unnatural. When energizing adrenaline gets added to the experience, your body unconsciously engages in these natural actions with extra vigor. More frequent rocking, shifting, pushing, brushing, fidgeting, and jingling make you look increasingly uncomfortable and unnatural. In the courtroom—where a certain level of formality and self-control is expected—the natural mannerisms that go unnoticed elsewhere appear conspicuous and unnatural. Thus the paradox! Clearly, "being natural" is the wrong method for discovering your personal style.

Your Brain

Another example of this paradox relates to your thought process. How often do you turn to someone you know well and ask questions to which you already know the answer? When was the last time you asked a good friend or colleague an extended series of questions beginning with, "What's your name? Where do you live? Are you married?" If you asked such questions, your friend would think you were suffering from temporary amnesia. Because you already know the answers, such questions seem decidedly odd.

Yet those are precisely the questions you ask your witnesses during direct examination. You ask questions to which you know the answers—indeed, *only* questions to which you know the answers. Your questions must be worded correctly, asked with appropriate curiosity, and sound spontaneous. Your examination should be as effortless as a natural conversation, not scripted and rehearsed.

Your Voice

You must be able to speak loudly enough for your voice to fill the courtroom. If you are a soft-spoken person by nature, this may feel completely unnatural to you. Yet, should the judge bark, "Counsel, speak up. We can't hear you!" you can't respond, "Sorry, your honor, that wouldn't be natural for me." Authoritative audibility is required in advocacy, whether it is natural for you or not. Further, you must be able to control the pace at which you speak; rid your speech of "thinking noises;" assess how emphatic your most persuasive arguments are; and choose the right word when the pressure is on. The ability to make conscious decisions about using your voice and speaking with finesse is a job requirement for trial lawyers.

Technique

Clearly, just "being yourself" won't make you a persuasive advocate, nor will instructing yourself to "be natural." To discover your authentic, personal style, you need a solid technique that will provide you with reliable answers to all those challenging questions about how to look, sound, and feel natural in the courtroom. How you control your body influences your ability to use your brain to think clearly and your voice to speak persuasively. As you develop and refine this technique, you pass through self-consciousness to self-awareness, and finally, to self-control. Once you have mastered a technique, the skills of trial advocacy become second nature.

CHAPTER ONE

Your Body

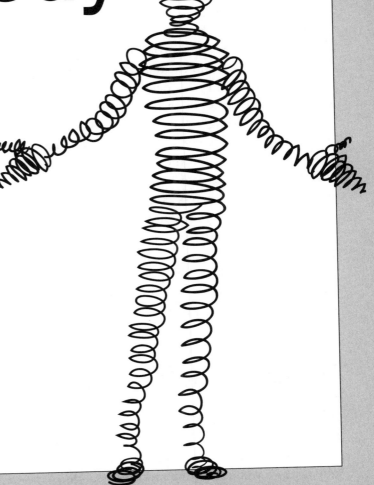

For trial lawyers, the name of the game is to look confident, comfortable, and credible in the courtroom. The way you stand, move, breathe, gesture, and focus your gaze in court significantly affects how a jury perceives you. As jurors listen to what you say, they scrutinize your physical behavior and judge your credibility. If your demeanor signals nervousness and discomfort, you won't be convincing. But if you act confident and enthusiastic in your role as zealous advocate, you will be persuasive. To achieve this initial goal—looking dynamically at ease and believable at all times, even when feeling nervous—requires a fail-safe technique for controlling your body.

Understanding the function of adrenaline is vital to this process, as few things have greater impact on an attorney's performance in court. Feelings of anxiety and excitement inevitably trigger the flow of adrenaline, which sends excess energy coursing through your system. This leads many advocates to pace or sway, breathe fast and shallow, gesture awkwardly, and fidget with their hands. Even the eyes are affected by adrenaline. Nervous energy makes it hard for the eyes to focus, and they tend to flit around the courtroom, depriving the jury of eye contact and the advocate of concentration. By learning to control your legs, breath, arms, hands, and eyes, you can channel this adrenaline and command how your body responds to it.

With guided practice, you will discover how to instruct your body to act in an appropriate and effective way. You can gain conscious control of your body by making desired behaviors part of a performance ritual. You will look comfortable and confident from the very beginning of every courtroom presentation, regardless of how you may feel.

Understanding Adrenaline

Adrenaline is a natural hormone dispensed by the adrenal glands. It flows through the body when your instinct detects a need for extra energy. This additional energy may be needed to help defend yourself, run away, or respond to the pressure of performance.

Performance pressures often take a positive form, such as excitement or anticipation. When athletes talk of "being pumped" for the big game, they are responding to that adrenaline being pumped, literally, by their bodies in anticipation of performance. Adrenaline also assists athletes by producing the extra energy needed to throw a ball farther or run faster, and by helping them to concentrate and focus the mind in the heat of competition. Likewise, adrenaline can be a positive factor in courtroom performance.

The body also pumps adrenaline in response to negative pressures, such as nervousness, anxiety, and panic. Excess nervous energy often is referred to as the fight-or-flight syndrome, because adrenaline energizes and animates muscles in our arms to help us fight and in our legs to help us flee.

Although our need to outrun predators has been reduced in modern society, thankfully, we're all familiar with adrenaline-induced energy: it makes your limbs tremble. If you stand up to speak and feel your hands shaking, this is the result of adrenaline preparing your arm muscles to fight. If you feel your knees knocking, adrenaline is pumping extra energy into your thighs and quadriceps to prepare you to run from a threat. The trembling occurs because every muscle in the body is paired with another muscle—for example, biceps and triceps work together to move your forearm—and when adrenaline energizes both simultaneously, the muscles tense and pull against each other, causing the arms or legs to shake.

The common form of nervousness known as "having butterflies in your stomach" occurs in muscles of respiration. The flutter of those metaphorical butterflies occurs when the diaphragm and intercostal muscles in the ribs pull against each other in response to adrenaline. As you speak, you feel a flutter, which sometimes becomes audible. Your voice shakes or cracks when this excessive muscular tension robs you of adequate breath support, without which you will not be loud enough to be heard. Chances are good you will be so distracted by these butterflies that you won't be your most articulate, persuasive self.

For many speakers, adrenaline pumps because of an ever-shifting balance between excitement and nervousness. It is not only invigorating to confront the challenge of speaking effectively, it is nerve-wracking—often just a little, sometimes quite a lot. Even experienced trial lawyers admit they experience this phenomenon. Although it is impossible to predict how much adrenaline you will generate at any given moment, it is guaranteed that you will feel the effect of at least *some* adrenaline. Regardless of its source, the secret is to channel adrenaline's corresponding energy in the most effective and appropriate way.

Adrenaline Overdose

An obviously nervous lawyer steps to the well of the courtroom to deliver his opening statement. He refers to a pre-admitted document as he moves awkwardly to counsel table. "During this trial, you will get to read this letter," he proclaims with quavering voice. When he picks it up and attempts to read it, the adrenaline in his arm causes the letter to shake visibly and audibly. Surprised, he emits an involuntary yelp and drops the document, which floats down to the table.

Bending over, he squints to read the letter from a safe distance and continues, "The letter says…"

Adrenaline's energy cannot be wished away simply by telling yourself to "Relax!" It must be channeled and released through the intentional use of stance, breath, gesture, and focus.

Helpful hint: Don't pick up a document until later in your presentation, after any adrenaline buzz has dissipated.

If adrenaline isn't channeled and released, it triggers various inappropriate, unconscious mannerisms that make you look and feel ill at ease. However, if you learn to recognize the impulses to fight, flee, or freeze, you can counter adrenaline's negative effects.

You can manage adrenaline's effects by getting control of specific parts of your body. Establish conscious control of your behavior using several seconds of silence after you stand up but before you begin to speak. You may feel an extra rush of adrenaline as you stand to face your judge, jury, or witness. During this silence, run through a short physical checklist in order to prepare your body and focus your mind. In the same way, Olympic athletes use an anticipatory silence to prepare to dive into a pool, ski down a mountain, or race around a track.

The Ultimate Ritual

In 1992, a 72-year-old retired chiropodist walked onto a basketball court in Riverside, California, and threw 2,750 consecutive free throws without a miss. Dr. Tom Amberry had such confidence in his technique that he brought along 10 witnesses who signed affidavits for his submission to the *Guinness Book of World Records.* Dr. Amberry readily admits he is not a great athlete and never was. So how did he accomplish such a feat? He had a great technique. In his book *Free Throw: 7 Steps to Success at the Free Throw Line,* he describes the mental and physical ritual that gave him such astonishing control and consistency.

Every move Dr. Amberry made prior to each throw of the ball was part of an unvarying ritual. During the silence before he threw the ball, he went through a physical checklist. How he planted his feet, how he breathed, how many times he bounced the ball, how his fingers held the ball, how he focused his eyes on the basket—every move was precisely the same 2,750 times. Because his ritual was so consistent, he achieved a remarkable result on the basketball court.

The lesson: Amberry's amazing feat, consistent ritual, and other discoveries of sports psychology can help you achieve similar success in the courtroom.

Controlling Your Body

Sports psychologists teach that if you want to perform at a high level, you need a consistent mental and physical ritual on which to base your performance. The function of this ritual is to enable the mind, through repetition and practice, to control the body, and to enable the body to control the mind. Together, body and mind help control emotion.

To achieve a consistently effective style, devise and refine a physical ritual for use every time you stand up in court, just like Dr. Amberry did on the basketball court. With practice, this ritual becomes "second nature"—behavior that looks natural, but is actually the result of technique, ritual, and diligent practice.

Reliance on a physical ritual frees your brain's prefrontal cortex (the area of your brain responsible for higher intellectual function) from being distracted by pacing, fidgeting or gesturing, and ensures that your body's actions will be governed by your motor cortex, the brain's overseer of natural automatic functions. Hence, by ritualizing your physical actions, you have engaged your instinct to move and gesture naturally. Your prefrontal cortex can then focus on more important things, such as what you want to say and how you want to say it.

Devise your own ritual, starting with your feet and moving up the body to your head. Use a mental checklist to position and align your body: feet, knees, hips, breath, arms, hands, shoulders, neck, head, face, and eyes. Running through this quick checklist will help you get control of your body, positioning and aligning yourself for optimum performance every time you stand up in court.

☐ Eyes

☐ Face

☐ Head

☐ Neck

☐ Shoulders

☐ Hands

☐ Arms

☐ Breath

☐ Hips

☐ Knees

☐ Feet

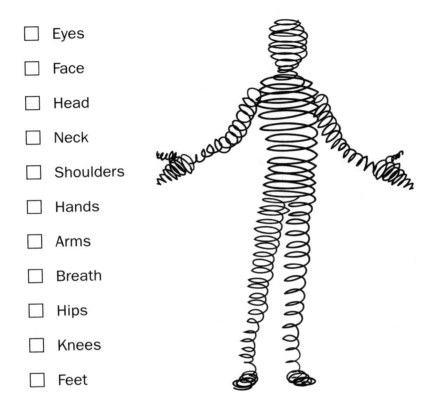

Think from the bottom up, focusing briefly on each part of your body. As you read about this ritual checklist, become conscious of the details of your alignment. Use your own body as a mnemonic device to memorize your physical ritual.

Plant Your Feet

In most sports, athletes start by planting their feet in the proper stance. The golfer adopts a stance and then swings a club. The baseball player ritualistically plants both feet in the batter's box and then swings a bat. The basketball player finds a stance on the free throw line and then throws. As a trial advocate, begin by planting your feet on the court-room floor.

Stand with your feet a comfortable distance apart. Don't place your feet so close together that your shoes touch; this stance is too narrow for a solid, comfortable foundation. Do not adopt a stance that is too wide or you will look like a gunslinger in a Western. Somewhere between the extremes of too narrow and too wide is a stance that is just right. Avoid standing with your feet in perfect parallel position, as if you are gliding along on skis. Such perfect symmetry can make you look slightly square and wooden, like a soldier at attention. Instead, try planting one foot—whichever one feels comfortable—an inch or two ahead of the other, with your feet slightly asymmetrical and out of alignment with each other. Slight asymmetry of the stance makes the body look more relaxed. Stand up right now and experiment to find the right stance. Better yet, stand in front of a floor length mirror so you can see how your stance looks. Once you are satisfied, use it every time you stand up in court. Soon it will become second nature, and your body, just like an athlete's, will do it automatically, without your needing to think about it.

Planting your feet happens in the moment before you speak. Do not utter a word until you have planted your feet and are standing still. Then, take another moment to pause, take a breath, and feel the floor.

Advocating Versus Acting

Actors on a stage do not think on their feet in the way advocates in the courtroom must. Actors recite lines they have memorized and rehearsed over many weeks of rehearsal. That is a very different cognitive and physical skill from advocacy.

Exactly how different was revealed when an Academy Award-winning actress starred in a Tennessee Williams play on Broadway. She gave an ethereal performance, and for over two hours revealed her consummate ability to communicate using her voice and her body.

But after the play she stepped out of character to deliver a curtain speech asking the audience to contribute to Broadway

Cares/Equity Fights AIDS. Although it was a short speech, she did not have it memorized. Instead, she pulled out a piece of paper, from which she read too quickly, and with numerous mistakes and dysfluencies. The physical prowess she had demonstrated so ably all evening vanished. She shifted nervously as she read, and by the end was standing with her legs crossed and feet a full 12" apart, looking as if she desperately needed to visit the bathroom. This talented woman had (literally!) stepped outside of her area of expertise, and when she should have spoken directly to her audience, she didn't have a technique for it.

Remember: Acting and advocacy are fundamentally different challenges. You don't need to win the Oscar® to win your case.

Stand Still

Newton's first law of motion also applies to trial advocacy: *A body at rest tends to remain at rest; a body in motion tends to remain in motion.* When you plant your feet and stand still, you look calm, comfortable, and in control, and your body will tend to stay at rest. If you start talking while your feet are still moving, your body tends to stay in motion, and may never stop. Random movement will make you appear nervous and ill at ease. Because adrenaline energizes your leg muscles, it is natural—but undesirable—to rock unconsciously, sway, pace, or shuffle your feet. So obey Newton's Law: plant your feet and stand still at the beginning of a presentation.

Flexible Knees

The next step in the ritual is to align and balance your knees and hips over your feet. Your knees should feel flexible. Don't lock your knees by pushing them backward, tightening the thigh muscles and drawing your kneecaps upward. The desirable sensation of flexibility is a feeling of the knee joint floating perfectly balanced. Think of it as "subway knees," similar to the adjustment the knees make when standing on public transportation as the door closes and the bus or subway car is about to move. If the subway is crowded and you have nothing to hold onto for balance, you flex your knees ever so slightly to maintain your balance when the car begins to move. The adjustment is subtle and virtually invisible. The knees do not bend as in a crouch, but adjust enough to flexibly absorb the forward lurch of the train as it pulls out of the station. With flexible knees your legs will feel comfortable, even when standing still for long periods of time.

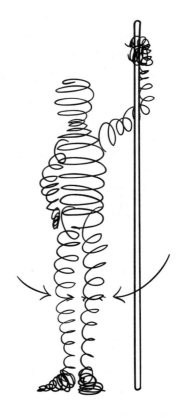

Stand up and experiment briefly to find this subtle feeling. Lock your knees backward and feel the sensation you want to avoid. Crouch slightly to move the knees in the opposite direction. Now find the perfect midpoint where the knee joint is floating and flexible. On the checklist, add these flexible knees to your planted feet as you continue to move up your body.

Center Your Hips

Center your hips over your feet and knees. This balances the weight of your torso evenly over both legs, allowing each leg to share the load equally. Although it may temporarily feel comfortable to stand with your body weight and hips shifted off to one side, this off-center position puts most of your body's weight onto a single leg. Eventually that leg gets tired and your body shifts the weight to your other leg. Soon your body is rocking side to side, as each leg in turn tires and shifts the burden to the other. This rocking motion distracts the jury and makes you look nervous.

Always start with your hips and body weight centered. If you feel your weight shift to one side, simply shift your weight back to center again and be still. Never rock and sway repetitively, but note that some looseness and flexibility of the body is desirable. You shouldn't feel as if you've been sunk in concrete. So avoid both repetitive rocking and absolute rigidity.

For women wearing high heels, be aware that they can subtly shift your weight forward onto your toes, causing the buttocks to shift backwards and up. This position shortens and tenses the muscles of your lower back. To counteract this, consciously center the pelvis over your feet and rotate it forward slightly—dancers refer to this as "tucking the tail bone." This will lengthen and relax the muscles in your lower back.

Once you have planted your feet, softened your knees, and centered your hips, you have conscious control of the biggest muscles of your body: buttocks, thighs, and calves. This allows you to control your adrenaline and stand still, even if you are feeling nervous. When you first stand in court, start by standing still, and then later on make a conscious decision about when and where to move, assuming the judge allows it. Some judges insist that lawyers remain standing behind a lectern unless they need to approach the witness stand with an exhibit. In some jurisdictions you must stay at a lectern so a microphone can record the proceedings. If that is what the situation demands, you must be able to comply comfortably. If a judge allows you the freedom to move, do so with a purpose.

Move with A Purpose

Your movement in the courtroom is completely at the discretion of the judge. Some judges require that you ask permission every time: "May I approach the witness, your honor?" Others may give you more general permission to move as you wish. Know what your judge will allow and adjust your behavior accordingly. Assuming you have permission to move, make it conscious and purposeful.

A purposeful move is motivated by and connected to your words and ideas. A purposeful move occurs when you walk to a new location as you move to a new topic: "Mr. Gomez, we've talked about your educational background, now I want to move on and focus on your professional experience." Or, "We've talked about your inventions and patents, now I want to ask you about your licensing agreement with the defendant." Once you move to a new location and start the new topic, stay there until you are finished and have asked all your questions about it. This purposeful use of movement assists the jury by helping to clarify the structure of your presentation. The move signals a new beginning, and may recapture the attention of jurors whose minds have wandered. It invites the distracted listener to re-engage.

Your decision to move must always be made by the thinking brain, not the adrenalized leg muscles. When the largest muscles in the body are energized by adrenaline, they move of their own accord. Powered by instinct and hormones, such movement is truly natural—but it doesn't make you look natural, and it certainly isn't desirable. Random movement may feel good because it uses and dissipates the adrenaline in your legs. But resist random movement, and move only when it makes sense, not because it feels good.

Movement has power if it starts from stillness, because the change from stasis to motion attracts attention. Incessant pacing robs movement of its impact. Don't be fooled into believing that constant movement keeps jurors interested. And don't be misled by the frequent movement you see in courtroom dramas on television. Actors pretending to be lawyers move frequently because the director knows that movement makes the camera shots more interesting. When the actor moves, the camera pans along with him, giving the shot visual variety. The camera does the work, not the viewer. The television stays in place and the viewers' eyes don't move much at all. In an actual courtroom, jurors forced to watch a pacing lawyer have to do the work of the camera, panning back and forth as if watching a ball in a tennis match. They tire quickly of tracking a moving target.

Aimless pacing creates visual monotony. The constant back and forth, rhythmic as a hypnotist's watch, can put juries to sleep. When you pace back and forth, you spend half your time with your back to half of the jury. Every time you turn around and pace in the opposite direction, you turn your back on some of your jurors. They will get bored with looking at your backside rather than your face. It is better to plant your feet and stand still in a central location facing the jury. When you make a purposeful move to a new location, stand still once again. Jurors can see your face and you can look them in the eye and tell them the truth. Sustained eye contact is impossible if you pace back and forth, and eye contact is a key element of persuasive style.

Vs and Ws

After hearing Marsha Hunter's communication lecture, a colleague told her about a course he had taken to prepare him for classroom teaching. He had learned this rule about public speaking: *Do not pace back and forth in front of the class. Instead, pace in patterns that make Vs and Ws, almost like a figure skater tracing shapes on the ice.* He was instructed, in effect, to vary his pacing by advancing on the class first and then retreating. By moving diagonally (tracing the V and W shapes) rather than straight back or straight forward, he would prevent any visual monotony for his listeners.

This is a non-solution to a real problem. How absurd to concoct a variation on pacing! That's like trying to cure the problem of saying *um* by mixing in *uh* and *er* so your listeners won't be so annoyed. Why not use the self-control required to trace Vs and Ws, and learn to stand still instead? That skill is a crucial part of speaking effectively.

Helpful hint: Don't be misled by silly solutions to real technical challenges. The discipline required to stand still is part of the task of effective persuasive speaking.

How much movement you use is very much a matter of personal style (and the judge's discretion). There are excellent trial lawyers who rarely move, while other, equally effective advocates move frequently. Make logical decisions about when and where you will move. Choose the topic areas—usually the most important ones—where you plan to move, in order to signal a transition into that discussion. Plan the moves in advance and practice to make sure they work for you. Movement is a stylistic choice, but it is neither a necessity nor a requirement for effective advocacy. If movement doesn't feel right to you, don't bother.

Once you have mastered the ability to plant your feet, float the knees, center the hips, stand still, and move with a purpose, you have conscious control of your body from your waist down to your feet. You are in control of your position in the courtroom. The next step is to focus on the middle of your body—the lower torso—where deep breathing occurs.

Conscious, Controlled Breathing

One of the most useful techniques for an advocate to ritualize is also the simplest: breathe consciously. The way you breathe is directly related to the way you feel, speak, and think. Once you learn to consciously control your breathing, it will help you calm down, project your voice, and oxygenate your brain. These three significant benefits flow from controlling how you breathe.

The technique of using breath to control emotions is widely understood. When someone is upset we often say, "You're upset—take a deep breath." Indeed, a few deep breaths have a calming effect because breath and emotion are directly connected. When we are relaxed and at ease we breathe with longer inhalations and longer exhalations. When we are nervous, anxious, or panic-stricken, adrenaline accelerates our rate of breathing.

Right now you are breathing unconsciously as you read this book. If you consciously accelerate the speed of your breathing while reading this sentence, you will begin to feel this connection between breath and emotion. Do it: breathe faster and shallower. The faster you breathe, the more it triggers an emotional response. Now breathe even faster and louder as you continue to read, and begin to simulate the respiratory action of panic. The action begins to provoke the feeling. If you breathe as if you are nervous (fast and shallow), you begin to feel nervous. No wonder—you're hyperventilating!

Fortunately, the reverse is also true. If you consciously breathe as if you are comfortable and at ease (even when you're not), the action of your conscious breathing can help to control your nervousness. If you take long, deep breaths, as you would while lying on a lawn chair on vacation, you can provoke the feeling of greater comfort. You breathe like you feel, and you feel like you breathe. If you consciously breathe using longer inhalations and exhalations, you imitate the action of your body's respiratory system when you are most comfortable. Take a few deep, relaxing, conscious breaths as you continue reading. Feel the difference.

The action of deeper, deliberate breathing provokes the feeling of greater comfort. While this technique does not make nervousness vanish, it can help take the edge off the anxiety you may feel sitting in the courtroom.

When you are breathing naturally, your respiratory system is controlled by your autonomic nervous system. This is the same system that regulates your beating heart, blinking eyes, and other vital functions. But you can override the autonomic nervous system at any moment, and take conscious control of your respiratory system. When you do so, conscious breathing calms you down and you feel better.

The Mechanics of Conscious Breathing

Your lungs are located in your upper torso, protected by your ribcage. Your diaphragm, which does most of the work of breathing, is a dome-shaped muscle underneath the lungs and atop the vital organs in the lower torso. When you draw a breath into your lungs, your diaphragm muscle flattens downward toward your waist, creating a partial vacuum that pulls air into your lungs. When the diaphragm moves down, the abdominal wall moves forward and the intercostal muscles pull the rib-cage outward slightly. As your lungs fill with air your internal organs are pushed down and forward as the diaphragm flattens. This is why a deep breath happens in the lower torso, even though your lungs are in your upper torso. It is your abdominal wall or belly that moves forward during deep breathing. When you take a deep breath, you should feel your stomach push forward gently against the belt or waistband of your clothing. This is not a large movement; don't be surprised at how subtle it is. Note also that the shoulders do not rise as the lungs expand. Only heavy exertion causes the upper torso and shoulders to heave up and down.

To feel the full power of this conscious, deep breathing, try this exercise. Draw a breath deeply into your lungs. Now empty your lungs and try to blow out every molecule of air as you exhale. Make an effort to completely empty your lungs. Keep blowing out until you feel an almost desperate need to inhale again, and then blow out the last little bit of air. Finally, when your lungs feel completely empty, breathe in. Feel the air rush back into your lungs. That is a truly deep, maximum breath. Try it again: empty your lungs as you exhale and then feel the air rush back in as you inhale. Activate the muscles of respiration that need to work long and hard when you speak in the courtroom. While you won't empty your lungs like this in court, it is important to understand that they have a surprising amount of untapped capacity you can use. Consciously exploit it.

The sooner you get conscious control of your breath, the better you feel. Do not wait until you have walked to the well of the courtroom to think about your breathing. Get control far in advance of that moment. A few minutes before you stand up, as you realize opposing counsel is ending her examination, take several conscious, deep breaths. Better still, take those conscious breaths hours earlier. As you walk up the courthouse steps, take a few deep breaths. As you drive to the courthouse, periodically inhale and exhale slowly, three times. When the alarm goes off in the morning and you feel that first rush of adrenaline as you think of the day's trial, take a few deep, deliberate breaths before you get out of bed.

Don't Freeze

Adrenaline is the fight-or-flight chemical, handed down over evolutionary time to help us stand our ground or get the heck out of the way during an emergency. The third f-word spawned by adrenaline is *freeze*.

Freezing is a defense tactic commonly used by animals in danger. Have you ever seen a rabbit "hiding" in the middle of your yard? Or a squirrel clutching the trunk of a tree, frozen in place? When they perceive a threat, they freeze, hoping the color of their fur acts as effective camouflage, and that predators will pass by without seeing them. But if the predator gets too close, rabbits and squirrels will move to their next tactic: flight. The rabbit quickly zigzags into the bushes; the squirrel shimmies up the tree and out of sight. Freezing temporarily bought time to assess the threat.

Humans under the influence of adrenaline also can freeze. When we do, we often don't realize what is happening. We may fail to move on to a new strategy when we should. When we freeze, we hold our breath—and on rare occasions, freezing can lead to passing out.

An articulate, personable, and energetic young woman rose to speak to a large group. She spoke from a pulpit. As she settled into position, she grabbed the sides of this massive piece of furniture with a white knuckle grip, and adrenaline's freeze impulse took hold. When she began to speak, her breath was fast and shallow. Her voice quavered and got weaker; her eyelids fluttered. She wobbled and swayed slightly, and it became obvious to the audience that she was about to faint. Six hundred people gasped in unison—which is a remarkable noise!

Fortunately, the two speakers seated behind her on the dais heard this collective gasp and leaped up to steady her as she fell backwards gracefully. Indeed, this hapless victim of adrenaline's freeze impulse had passed out.

Helpful hint: Breathe consciously to mitigate adrenaline's stronger effects, which include the impulse to freeze, rabbit-like, in place. Breathe consciously to remain standing!

Conscious breathing is also an excellent way to short-circuit the fretting about the future that plagues many advocates far in advance of standing up in court. If you find yourself spiraling down into an anxiety attack, stop yourself with the instruction: *Breathe consciously right now.* Conscious breathing in the present moment distracts you from thinking about the future, over which you have no control.

If you sing in a choir or play a wind instrument, you may have used a similar technique to achieve deep, conscious breathing, which is also known as abdominal or belly breathing. Practitioners of yoga and martial arts use conscious or mindful breathing deep in the torso; athletes learn to exploit deep breathing as part of the ritual of preparing for competition. Likewise, mindful breathing will improve your performance in the courtroom.

Breathe In and Speak Out

Once you use conscious, deliberate breathing to feel better, you can use that same breathing to achieve your second goal: speaking better. Chapter Three will describe more completely the connection between breathing and speaking, but it is important to mention the subject here as part of the physical ritual of preparation.

Stage actors and singers refer to the connection between breathing and speaking on the stage as "breath support." The amount of air in your lungs is what supports and projects your voice in court. Your voice is loud in direct proportion to the volume of air in your lungs. Less air means less sound; more air means more sound. If you take conscious control of your breath while still sitting at counsel table, you then have more air available when you stand up to speak. If you are naturally soft-spoken, there is only one way to turn up the volume: use more air as you speak. If you need more air flowing out of your lungs to speak louder, you obviously must bring more air into your lungs with each inhalation. That air is then available to put more power behind your voice.

You speak on the exhalation of breath from the lungs. Patsy Rodenburg, the preeminent voice coach at London's Royal National Theatre, describes the mechanics of speaking as "breathe in, speak out." Breathe in to fill your lungs. Then speak as the air flows back out. The breath flows up and past your voice box or trachea, where your vocal cords are made to vibrate by the passing air. Start speaking when your lungs are full of air. Don't make the mistake of inhaling, exhaling, and then trying to speak. Breathe in, and speak out once you have filled your lungs with air.

Oxygenate Your Thinking Brain

You will discover a third benefit of conscious breathing. The more efficiently you breathe, the more you increase the amount of oxygen in your lungs, which passes into your bloodstream and circulates throughout your body—including to your brain. Your brain needs about 20% of the oxygen your body takes in. The more efficiently and deeply you breathe, the more ample the supply of oxygen to your lungs, your bloodstream, and ultimately, your brain. This will help you to think quickly and clearly.

Since conscious breathing will help you feel better, speak better, and think better, the sooner you begin the process of conscious breathing and the more consistently you do it, the more control you will have. Just as planting your feet and standing still controls the adrenaline in your legs, controlling the breath prevents adrenaline from accelerating your respiration.

The next challenge is to channel and release adrenaline's considerable energy, allowing it to flow appropriately out of the body; for that you need to use your arms, hands, and shoulders.

What Do You Do with Your Hands?

This is the million dollar question that many advocates struggle with. There are different ways to answer it. Since you want to look and feel natural in court, it may seem logical to tell yourself to simply gesture the way you always do. But that answer is not helpful, because of the paradox of naturalness discussed in the Introduction. You don't know what your own gestures look like. "Gesture naturally" is at best a partial answer.

A common answer to this question of what to do with your hands is, "Don't gesture." Some people cling to an old-fashioned belief that gestures are inappropriate in court. Law students and attorneys are commonly told to place their hands on the lectern or at their sides, because gestures distract the jury, or worse, the judge. There are three problems with this belief: there is no scientific evidence to back it up; it is completely unnatural to inhibit your gestures; and it is not the way effective lawyers behave in court. If your goal is to be natural in court, then standing with your arms dangling at your sides or latching onto the lectern couldn't be a worse answer.

The assertion that gestures are distracting is an excellent example of unreliable hearsay. Neuroscientists and social scientists who study gestures have discovered that gesture and language are inextricably intertwined in the human brain. Research in the areas of neurology and cognition proves beyond a reasonable doubt that gesturing is an integral component of speaking and thinking. You must gesture in order to look, feel, speak, and think naturally in the courtroom. Gestures not only enhance the meaning of language, they allow the body to channel and release the energy of adrenaline.

Everyone gestures. Some people do it more and others less, but everyone gestures in conversation, especially when speaking persuasively. Reading this, you may be saying to yourself, "But I don't gesture! I know I don't gesture." You may not be aware of it—yet—because your gestures are not controlled by the conscious intellect. They are controlled by instinct.

But I Don't Gesture!

An advocate comes to video review, determined to prove that she really doesn't gesture. Although she had just heard a lecture emphasizing that everyone gestures in conversation, she is sure she is the exception. As she argues that she does not gesture, she is, of course, gesturing as she speaks! The instructor begins, "It is curious you should say that, because you just gestured everything you said to me about not gesturing."

Clearly frustrated at the observation, she sits down, trapping one hand to stifle the impulse to gesture, and watches the video of her opening statement. On the video she stands absolutely still with her hands in the classic fig leaf position, demurely clasped in front of her. The instructor stops the video to comment that she appears bored and uncomfortable. As she explains that she was taught to speak that way in court, she again gestures constantly as she talks; he again points this out. With increasing frustration she now sits on both hands to try and keep from gesturing as she speaks. Now she looks as uncomfortable off camera as she does on.

Why fight it? Everyone has an instinct to gesture. Use that instinct in the courtroom to be yourself—and be much more effective.

To better understand this principle, observe and analyze how people talk to one another. Start paying attention to your own gestures. What do you do with your hands during conversations with friends, family, and colleagues? Notice how often your hands move while you speak. How large are those movements? How long do the patterns of gesture last? Watch others, too. As you become increasingly aware of gestures, you will discover an amazing amount of communication literally right under your nose, and you never noticed it before.

The Science of Natural Gestures

After a trip to Italy, Dr. Jana Iverson was inspired to study the origin of gesturing. Her research posed the following questions: Do we learn to gesture by watching others do it? In other words, are gestures nurtured by observation and imitation when children are learning to speak? Or is it hard-wired in the human brain—is it nature rather than nurture that makes us gesture? Her research studied children who were blind from birth, observing them in conversation with others.

Dr. Iverson discovered something surprising. Congenitally blind children use gestures when they talk, even when speaking to other blind people. The blind children gestured the same as the sighted children in her control group. How can someone gesture who has never seen a gesture? Dr. Iverson's study reveals the innate connection in the brain between the flow of gestures and the flow of language. Dr. Iverson writes, "The fact that someone who had never seen gestures before would gesture, even to a partner who they know can't see, suggests that gesturing and speaking are tightly connected in some very fundamental way in our brains." Gestures not only help speakers speak, the flow of gestures also assists listeners in understanding what is being said.

The journal *Research on Language and Social Interaction* published a special issue called *Gesture and Understanding in Social Interaction* in 1994. The studies revealed the important connection between thinking, speaking, gesturing, and listening. In one study, people comprehended spoken sentences *twice as well* when gestures accompanied speech as when gestures were absent. In another study, the subjects (think: jurors) were told a short story (think: opening statement) and then given a partial transcript of the story and asked to fill in the missing parts. The researchers concluded: "…those parts of the story accompanied by well-defined gestures were filled in with greater accuracy." In other words, your gestures will help your jurors remember what you said.

Another study in this collection found that "people obtain information from gestures accompanying speech that they integrate with the information that is conveyed in the speech." Your gestures can provide jurors with important information. Other studies conclude that "gestures together with speech can provide the recipient with a more complete understanding of the utterance, that gestures sometimes may even provide a component that is crucial for its understanding." Gestures give subtle clues about intent and point of view, crucial components in comprehension, which allow your jury to better understand what you are saying. All the research points to this conclusion: if you want jurors to follow, remember, and be persuaded by what you are saying, you must gesture.

Gestures not only assist your jurors' understanding of what you are saying, they will help you remember what you intended to say and to say it better. Researcher Adam Kendon at the University of Pennsylvania asserts that gestures help speakers find the right words. Speakers use gestures to conjure the proper words from memory. The journal *Psychological Science* reported that Dr. Susan Goldin-Meadow of the University of Chicago found that people who were allowed to gesture while recalling a list of memorized words recalled on average 20% more than people who were not allowed to gesture. In other words, gesturing assists your word retrieval and memory. If gesturing will improve your ability to recall and remember what you want to say by a full 20%, it is obvious that gesturing is an essential element of your personal style.

Further scientific evidence of the close linkage between speech, gesture, and comprehension can be found in David McNeill's *Hand and Mind* as well as Dr. Susan Goldin-Meadow's *Hearing Gesture: How Our Hands Help Us Think*. Neurologist Frank R. Wilson's *The Hand: How its use shapes the brain, language, and human culture* provides an anthropological perspective to the issue.

Jump-Start Your Own Gestures

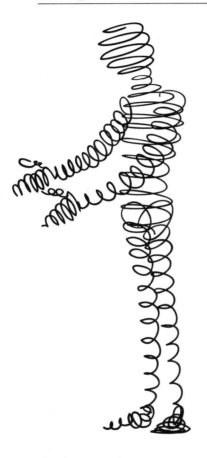

You have a lifetime of experience at gesturing. Instinctively and unconsciously, your body already knows how to gesture. But you need a technique to jump-start them from the beginning of every presentation. Think about your gestures to get them started, so you can stop thinking about them once they get going. The challenge is to immediately liberate your hands so they can move freely, and to avoid over-intellectualizing what they do every minute.

Triggering your natural gestures is analogous to jump-starting a dead car battery. You connect jumper cables from a working battery to the dead battery. The working battery jump-starts the dead one when you turn the key in the ignition. Once the engine is running, you remove the jumper cables, slam the hood, and drive off, confident that the battery will now do its job.

At the very beginning of a presentation, the instinct to gesture can be as dead as a car battery at twenty below zero, frozen by self-consciousness, anxiety, or the erroneous belief that gestures are distracting. To jump-start your gestures, think of your brain as the energy source. Connect the metaphorical jumper cables of conscious thought to your instinct to gesture and turn the key. Consciously gesture at the beginning, telling your arms and hands to move, even when the body resists. Make sure your gestural engine is running.

Get the Feel of It First

When learning how to finger the strings of a guitar, dance the tango, or swing a golf club, you may look and feel a little awkward at first, until you get the feel of it.

To learn a new physical skill, you begin by thinking intensely about the action required. That thinking takes place in the prefrontal cortex of your brain. When learning to play the guitar you have to deliberately think about each chord: put the index finger here, middle finger there, ring finger there, and the pinkie finger over here. You concentrate on each chord and make mistakes. Your playing feels awkward. But once you begin to get the feel of it, your motor cortex begins to control the action. Muscle memory places your fingers on the guitar strings. You think: C major chord, and your fingers know where to go.

This conscious gesturing may not feel natural the first time you try it. Don't be discouraged. The specific gestures you instruct your hands to make are natural, but the conscious activity of the brain telling the hands to do them is unnatural. It is technical, and first you need to learn and practice the mechanics. With enough practice it becomes second nature. Instead of learning a new skill such as golf or tennis, you are perfecting a technique for triggering your own natural gestures.

Remember: Gesturing is an essential element of an articulate style. Don't let a little initial awkwardness frustrate you. Practice the skill until you get the feel of it.

Even though you gesture in a unique personal style, there are some general observations that apply to everybody. These also aid our understanding of gestures. As you observe your gestures and those of other speakers, pay specific attention to how large the gestures are and how long they last. Note the specific shape of the hands while gesturing, and where hands go when they are still. Rather than focus on the faces of speakers, look at their hands.

The Zone of Gesture

Natural gestures have observable and quantifiable characteristics. For example, conversational gestures are surprisingly large. They move or

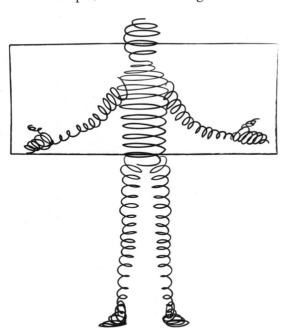

flow through an area in front of the body called the "zone of gesture." This zone is a large rectangular space approximately two feet tall by four feet wide. It extends vertically from the waist to the nose. Gestures rarely happen with the hands below the waist or above the shoulders. This zone extends horizontally about two feet out to each side of your body—almost the full reach of your arms. Even when you are sitting down, your gestures regularly fill this zone.

When sitting in a mall, restaurant, or airport, watch the animated conversations taking place around you and note the size of the gestures you see. When sitting in a meeting and listening to others speak, focus on hands. Watch how people gesture on television and in films. Watch television with the sound turned off to observe gestures. You will be surprised at how large natural gestures really are. As the title of Dr. Susan Goldin-Meadow's book suggests: start *hearing* gestures. Listen to the words people are saying, but watch their hands. Observe the size of the zone of gesture, and see the obvious connection between speech and gesture.

Natural gestures involve the whole arm from the shoulder to the hand. This isn't to suggest that all gestures are large and expansive; many are not. But all gestures naturally use the entire limb. Extend your arms so your gestures comfortably fill the zone of gesturing. When you feel some "air in your armpits," you'll know your gestures are large enough.

By using your whole arm, you avoid a common pitfall of nervous speakers: gesturing with just wrists or forearms. Anxious advocates keep the upper arms tight against the body, as if the elbow has been bolted to their ribcage. This not only shrinks the zone of gesture, it limits the size of gestures, making them appear and feel unnatural. Their smaller gestures look tight and jerky; the zone of gesture is shrunken and cramped. The body's instinct for self-preservation keeps the hands and forearms in front of vital organs for protection, making gestures tentative and constricted. Such half-gestures merely reveal a speaker's anxiety, doing nothing to clarify the meaning of speech. They don't last long enough to support and reinforce expressive speaking. Such constricted gestures usually happen comically fast, like "Benihana gestures" which mimic the lightning-fast moves of knife-wielding chefs at those Japanese restaurants.

In addition to being large and filling the zone of gesture, natural gestures often last a long time. Watch how many seconds a pattern of conversational gesturing stays active and animated, unlike such relatively short-lived actions as a clenched fist, the obscene flip of "the bird," or the circular thumb and index finger indicating "okay." (These iconic and culturally specific gestures differ fundamentally in duration from the flowing patterns of conversational gesturing.) It is not uncommon for people to simultaneously talk and gesture nonstop for many minutes, especially when speaking energetically and persuasively. In fact, speaking energetically and persuasively *requires* gestures that are long, smooth, and loose.

The Impulse to Gesture

When language needs emphasis but emphatic gestures are suppressed (whether by nervousness or a belief that gesture is inappropriate), the instinct surfaces in some inappropriate way. It can reveal itself in the twitch of a finger, the flick of a wrist, or a quick flap of a forearm. These are not complete gestures, but an impulse or attempt, revealing that the body is instinctively trying to gesture but is prevented from doing so by self-consciousness or nerves. When you observe these impulses carefully, you can see a direct correlation between the impulse and the words. The impulse is not just a nervous fidget; it shows the connection between speech and gesture in the brain. The hands know instinctively which words are important and need emphasis. The urge to gesture occurs particularly on those key words that clarify meaning.

When gestures are inhibited and reduced to twitching fingers and flapping forearms, listeners hear the result in verbal expression. When your gestures are restrained, your speech tends towards monotone. Ideas are not delivered clearly and emphatically because the gesture needed to accompany the word is absent or underpowered. Both your language and your listener suffer.

If you have doubts about how strong the impulse to gesture is, consider how often people plunge their hands into their pockets while speaking. Even tucked deep within, the hands don't stay still. They jingle change and continue to fidget. Look carefully at such speakers, and you can see the impulse to gesture transformed, spasming inside their pockets. The impulse to gesture doesn't go away—it is merely displaced, at times to the detriment of both message and speaker.

Beware of Pocket Puppets

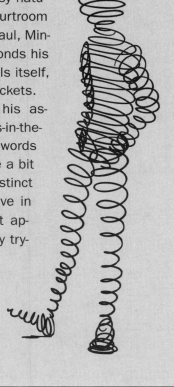

The senior partner stands to introduce the guest. He plunges both hands into pockets, attempting to capture a folksy naturalness. "Our speaker today is a courtroom communication consultant from St. Paul, Minnesota...," he begins, and within seconds his unconscious instinct to gesture reveals itself, even with his hands trapped in his pockets.

This gentleman is entertaining his associates unwittingly with a hands-in-the-pocket puppet show. As he speaks, words that deserve verbal emphasis receive a bit too much gestural emphasis. His instinct to gesture is alive and well and active in a painfully obvious way. Each pocket appears to hold a chipmunk desperately trying to escape.

Remember: Rather than stuffing your hands into pockets, have them in a ready position before you speak so your gestural instinct can flow immediately.

To sum up: when you begin to speak, make your initial gestures loose and smooth. Why do we say "Isn't she smooth?" to compliment a good speaker? Because it is literally true. Natural gestures are larger and longer than the constrained, short gestures of nervous speakers. They are also smooth instead of jerky, slow instead of fast. Given the interrelationship between gesturing, speaking and thinking, being literally smooth with your arms and hands will bring smoothness to your verbal delivery and mental flow.

What Do You Do with Your Hands When You Are Not Gesturing?

No one gestures all the time, not even avid gesticulators. Gestural flow alternates between action, when hands are moving, and stillness, when they are not. Your hands need a neutral position of readiness that can be used as part of your physical ritual checklist. If your hands are in a position where they are poised to gesture, your gestures will flow naturally.

The Ready Position

The concept of a ready position comes from watching experienced trial lawyers and asking the question, "Where do they put their hands when they are not gesturing?" Their hands regularly retreat to a position directly in front of the waist, and touch loosely. Hands and forearms are energized and ready to go, not pressed against the abdomen. The position is loose, not tight. A little bit of space separates the forearms from the abdomen.

Consider the logic of this position. In the ready position, the muscles of your upper arm hold a small amount of tension to keep the hands at waist height. Without that muscular tension, the hands drop below the waist to the classic "fig leaf" position, where they are placed modestly in front of the crotch. The fig leaf is the default, unready position of the nervous advocate. While the fig leaf is a perfectly natural resting position if waiting for an elevator or the ATM machine, this below-the-waist position leaves the arms and hands under-energized and unready to gesture. The instinct to gesture cannot begin to flow easily when the arms are hanging limply. Other positions that prevent gestures from flowing are the reverse fig leaf (hands clasped behind the back, or what the military calls "parade rest"), hands resting on the lectern, or leaning on counsel table. The ready position works because it places the hands in the same location where they do most of their work: in front of the body at waist height and poised for action.

Recall where your hands are when you hold and read a book—directly in front of the middle of your body. That is the same general location where arms and hands eat, read, write, compute, check your cell phone, or set your watch. If you want to gesture naturally, keep your hands where they spend the greatest amount of time working. For most people, the ready position puts hands right in front of the belly button, with biceps slightly energized and elbows bent at ninety degrees. Here, they are also right at the bottom of the zone of gesture that extends vertically from waist to nose. By placing your hands in this position and returning to it when you are not gesturing, you will find it easier to trigger your instinct to gesture.

The "Invisible" Ready Position

Every time Brian Johnson lectures he says to his audience, "I've now been speaking to you for forty minutes. Raise your hand if you have noticed where I put my hands when I am not gesturing." How many hands go up? Often none at all, sometimes a few. It's a strange thing, but the ready position is invisible to most observers. When he walks closer to the folks in the front row, it's apparent that his hands in the ready position are precisely at the eye level of the listeners. Why then, is it virtually invisible?

Listeners focus on eyes, not hands. So you can trust that

your ready position—hands loosely touching in front of the belly button—will not be consciously seen by the fact finders listening to you. It's invisible.

Pay close attention to all sorts of speakers, both live or on television, and you will observe this ready position being used constantly—the local weatherman, David Letterman or Jay Leno on late-night television, the TV news reporter from the war zone. They all use it; you've just never noticed. See now what has been invisible to you before.

Remember: Use the ready position. No one will notice.

Never Say Never

Should you *never* place your hands in pockets, behind your back, in the fig leaf? Never say *never*. All those positions are viable options to be used occasionally. The question is—when? If you briefly place your hands in the fig leaf position, reverse fig leaf, in your pockets or on the lectern, that's okay. But be aware that once your hands retreat to one of these resting positions they will stay there longer than is desirable, because bodies at rest tend to stay at rest. Consciously avoid these resting positions at the beginning of a courtroom presentation. However, once you liberate your gestural instinct and get it going, it is perfectly acceptable for the hands to cycle through a wide variety of positions. Variety is the spice of life and of advocacy technique. When you are listening to a witness answer a question, the jury's eyes are focused on the witness, not you. Such moments as these are a perfect opportunity for the hands to adopt one of the alternative positions. Just don't get stuck there too long!

The Mechanics of Readiness

Your hands can touch each other in a number of ways in the ready position. It doesn't matter how, as long as you can keep them still and don't fidget. Wringing the hands—the cliché of nervousness—is the result of adrenaline energizing the hands to rub each other. Use this energy for gesturing instead. The important thing is that your hands remain still, yet ready for your gestures to be released and begin to flow. Do not rest your forearms snugly against your belly for extended periods of time. The point of the ready position is to start gesturing immediately. If you remain in the ready position too long, you will appear to have joined a religious order. Resist your body's impulse to interlace your fingers as if in prayer. You will find it difficult to separate your hands; even a little tension in those interlaced fingers will lock your hands together.

If you are long-waisted or have short arms, have an ample paunch or are pregnant, you may need to adjust your hands and arms higher or lower to suit your body type. Experiment to find a position where your elbows are still at 90 degrees, but your hands are open and ready to gesture. Try bringing your fingertips together, touching lightly. If you are pregnant and near full term, choose a ready position before it chooses you, as it did for the student whose hands gently rubbed her burgeoning belly during summation—providing a charming but ultimately embarrassing moment in classroom video review.

The Secret Handshake

One particularly useful ready position is the "secret handshake." It is especially helpful for extremely nervous speakers. To experiment with this position, hold your hands with both palms facing forward and extend the thumb of your right hand out to the side. With your left hand, gently grab your right thumb as if it were the handlebar of a bicycle. Pull your hands loosely toward your belly button, and position your hands so that you conceal the fact that you are holding onto your thumb. The secret handshake gives you a security blanket—a warm thumb to hold—yet it permits a quick release of that thumb to allow the gestures to flow. The secret handshake is far preferable to the common courtroom practice of holding a pen.

Don't Hold a Pen

A surprising number of advocates claim to feel more comfortable when they hold a pen while speaking. Why does a slender cylinder of plastic inspire such comfort and confidence? Holding a pen while speaking is illogical. It makes as much sense as holding a microphone while writing. Yet, silly as it is, holding a pen is a widely popular solution to the problem of what to do with your hands.

Obviously, if you need to write something down, pick up your pen and use it, but then put it down. That is what a pen is for—writing, not speaking. If you hold a pen you will inevitably distract the jury with it. You will click it, fondle it, twirl it, and stroke it. Unconsciously you will fidget with the pen, and this will prevent your gestures from flowing. The energy of adrenaline will animate your hands to play with your pen and annoy your jury.

What is the real reason that lawyers like to hold pens? It puts the hands into the ready position! People hold pens with both hands at waist height. So keep the ready position but get rid of the pen. The same applies to holding anything in your hands—marker pens, a computer remote control, laser pointers, and even eyeglasses. If you need a security blanket to hold onto, try the secret handshake instead. Put everything else down.

Some Gestures Are Distracting

Everyone has seen speakers whose gestures are distracting and even annoying. Distracting gestures differ fundamentally from natural gestures that are useful and effective. Repetitive gestures become monotonous and call attention to themselves. If you use the same gesture over and over, it becomes distracting. Such gestures merely keep beating tedious time in an annoying accompaniment to your verbal delivery. "Baton gestures," as they are called, make the speaker look like the mediocre conductor of an inept marching band.

Avoid falling into a gestural rut. Do not point at the jury with your index finger; it looks like you are nagging rather than persuading. Refrain from pointing repeatedly at the opposing party across the courtroom. Avoid the "thumb puppet," so popular among politicians, where the tip of the thumb sticks up over the index finger of a loose fist. Your credibility will not be enhanced if you look like a politician.

Trust that your natural gestures are not repetitive and monotonous. They are varied because they are inextricably connected to your words.

Three R's of Natural Gesture

As you practice gesturing, remind yourself to use the Three R's: *ready, release,* and *relax.* First, put your hands in the ready position so that they are *ready* to gesture. Assume this ready position before you speak, making it part of your physical ritual of preparation. The second R requires that you *release* your gestures as you begin talking and fill the zone of gesture. Don't wait; gesture immediately. (There is a discussion below about how to release your gestures.) As you speak, your hands and arms will be engaged in either *ready* or *release* most of the time. You *release* your gestures when you ask a question of a witness, then return to the ready position to listen to the answer. Sometimes for variety and comfort let your arms *relax*—the third R. Take all tension out of your arm muscles so the arms drop gently to your sides and hang there briefly.

Once you master the three Rs, you can combine *release* and *relax* to give yourself two additional options. While the right hand is gesturing, the left arm can be relaxed and hanging at your side. As the left hand gestures, the right arm relaxes. In other words, don't always gesture with both hands; the variety of ambidexterity is desirable. These options—right hand, left hand, and both hands—give you five different ways to use your arms while gesturing in the courtroom. Simply cycle through the five positions randomly, using *ready* and *release* most of the time, but occasionally letting one or both arms *relax*. Relax is an especially useful position to use when a witness is answering a question on direct examination.

If you experiment with the ready position and eventually discover that it doesn't work for you, use an alternative. Place your hands at your sides in the *relax* position as the neutral position when you are not gesturing. This looks fine. Be aware that since the arm muscles are hanging slack, it takes more conscious effort to start the gestures flowing.

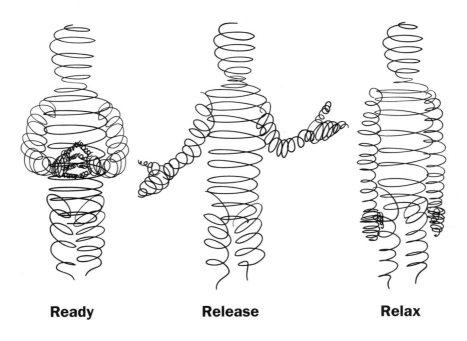

Ready   **Release**   **Relax**

Give, Chop, and Show

There are three types of gestures that everyone uses regularly in conversation. Once you have placed your hands in the ready position, consciously instruct your arms to release an initial gesture. Three simple words will help you remember your options: *give, chop,* and *show*. Practice them in private until you can use them with confidence in court.

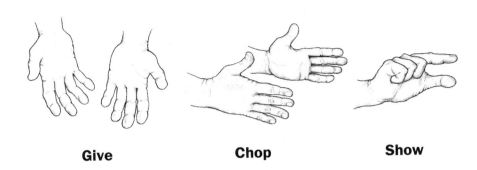

Give   **Chop**   **Show**

Give. When you give the jury a fact in opening statement, the hand appears to engage in the action of giving. The hand is open with palm facing upwards. Fingers are straightened and separated slightly, neither tensely squashed together nor splayed widely apart. Look at your own hand and do this palm-up gesture now. Use the give gesture and say:

Mr. Douma got to work at 8:30.

This gesture can be done with one or both hands.

The *give* gesture is especially useful in court because it is how you gesture when asking questions. When used with a question it becomes the *questioning gesture*. You appear to literally hand the question to the witness just as you would hand her a small object placed on your palm. Try the palms up questioning gesture with both hands and shrug your shoulders slightly. It is clear you are implying a question even if you don't say a word; this is universally understood body language.

Chop. When people speak and gesture emphatically, they turn their hands sideways as if using a gentle karate chop. This gesture is especially useful in closing argument or when asking important leading questions on cross examination. The *chop* gesture accompanies and intensifies a powerful verbal statement. This emphatic *chop* can be done with one or both hands. Hands are usually separated about body-width apart.

When the hands are separated even wid-
er than that, the *chop* is big, powerful
and authoritatively emphatic.

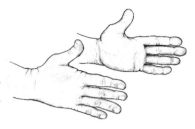

If you find yourself repetitively
pointing at the jury or a witness, simply
convert your pointing finger to the *chop*.
Uncurl and straighten the other four fingers. This turns your pointing
finger into the chopping hand of emphasis. No one takes offense if all
five fingers are pointing together; it is the index finger alone that is
bothersome.

Show. The show gesture is sometimes a literal enactment of your
words. As you speak, the hands recreate the literal action:

> I had my briefcase in my left hand, and as I reached for the railing
> with my right hand, I slipped on the stairs.

Like a visual aid, the hands *show* or demonstrate what the words are
describing. The left hand appears to grip the invisible briefcase handle;
the right hand reaches forward toward the railing. Read that statement
aloud and execute the mechanics of the gesture with your own hands to
get a feel for this idea. You gesture like this unconsciously all the time.
Sometimes the *show* gesture illustrates a concept yet still functions
as a visual aid for the listener. This sort of expression is common in
conversation:

> On one hand, *I'd like to go* to the party,
> but on the other hand, I'm so busy that *I really shouldn't.*

Using the *show* gesture in this example, gesture, "I'd like to go"
with one hand and "I really shouldn't" with the other hand. Each gesture *shows* the listener what we are talking about; in this case, contrast
between ideas. In conversation the listener might well respond, "I see
your dilemma." Gestures literally *show* a visualization that the listener
sees. Try it. Use your hands to show us the issue:

Who is at fault? The plaintiff (on the one hand) or the defendant (on the other hand)?

Get the feel for *show* with, "The car came within a few inches of hitting her trike," as in this illustration.

These three choices can trigger your instinct to gesture. Don't be surprised if initially it feels awkward to use *give*, *chop*, and *show* consciously. It takes practice to get the feel of it. Use the Three R's (*ready*, *release*, and *relax*) and the three gestures (*give*, *chop*, and *show*) to simplify the challenge of gesturing consciously. One last concept completes your gestural vocabulary.

Gesture "On the Shelf"

A useful method for understanding and jump-starting gestures is to imagine placing ideas "on the shelf." The vast majority of natural gestures take place at waist height, and this "shelf" is the bottom of the zone of gesture that extends from waist to nose. Therefore, every time you stand up to speak, there is an imaginary invisible shelf in front of you at waist height. When your hands are in the ready position, they are resting on this invisible shelf. It is always there in front of you, demarcating the bottom of your zone of gesture. When you observe conversational gestures, notice that they usually happen at about waist height or "on the shelf"—even when people are sitting down.

Whether you are giving, chopping, or showing, use the shelf analogy to help jump-start your gestures. For example, giving a question to a witness looks something like the action of placing a big fish on the shelf with both hands. You can also put the question on the shelf with one hand or the other for variety. Put this book down and make the two-handed give gesture right in front of your seated body at about waist height. Look at your hands. Then do it with one hand, and then the other. Say aloud, "Where were you on July 4th?" and use the questioning gesture on the shelf. Make it smooth by extending your hands forward as you say "Where," and leave them extended until you say

"July 4th." Give the whole question from start to finish.

When using the emphatic chop gesture, the invisible shelf is where a martial artist might break a board with a karate chop. Of course, you will not use the chop with such violence, but the chop happens on the waist-height shelf. If you were a prosecutor speaking to a jury you might say, "The defendant's *fingerprints* were on the *gun*." Say it aloud as if you believe it, with a chop gesture on the words fingerprints and gun.

Finally, the show gesture places ideas on this same shelf:

On the one hand *[placed on the shelf with the right hand]*,

I'd like to go to the party,

but on the other hand *[placed on the shelf with the left hand]*,

I'm so busy I really shouldn't.

Try those gestures with this statement:

The defendant is to blame; Nancy is not responsible.

Right now, practice several times to get the feel of it.

Summing Up Gestures

Your physical ritual prepares you to gesture. As you adopt your stance, center your body, take a conscious breath, and place your arms in the ready position before you speak. Immediately upon speaking, jump-start your instinct to gesture using give, chop, or show gestures, and place them on the shelf. Extend your arms so you have some "air in the armpits." This will help you find gestures that are slower, smoother, larger, and longer. You now have an answer to the question of what to do with your hands. Practice until it becomes second nature.

Posture and Alignment

Moving up the body, posture is the next topic. What is good posture? The answer most people learn as children turns out to be wrong.

Posture refers to the position or bearing of the body. We can all conjure in our mind's eye a vision of ideal posture: the body upright and erect, the head held high. Imagine an athlete poised for action, a dancer standing on a stage, or a line of soldiers at ease.

Surprisingly, the conventional wisdom you may have learned about how you achieve this proper posture is wrong. Slouching children are told to put their shoulders back and their chest out. But carrying tension in the shoulders and chest doesn't look or feel good. Instead, you look and feel tense because you are tensing the muscles of your upper torso. It is also difficult to maintain this so-called good posture, because it is downright uncomfortable.

Good posture comes from properly aligning your back, chest, shoulders, neck, and head. Your entire spine—which extends from your tailbone up into your skull—must be aligned to gracefully carry the torso, neck, and head over hips and legs. Good posture includes much more than just your shoulders and chest.

The misguided instruction to pull shoulders back and thrust the chest up is a response to a real and visible problem. Bad posture appears to be caused by the shoulders slouching forward, which makes the chest collapse. But the real problem begins above the shoulders and chest with the incorrect position of the neck and head.

Your Neck and Head

When you think about your own body, do you imagine that the back of your head shares the same plane as the back of your torso? If you could see yourself in profile, chances are that you would discover that your head and neck are positioned forward of your torso. Because you only see the front view of yourself in mirrors, you may be surprised at how far in front of your body you carry your head and neck. (That is, unless you studied ballet for years or have recently served in the military!) People with very poor posture have necks that angle out from the shoulders at 45 degrees, with the head perched way out ahead of the torso. When you watch a crowd of people parade past you, observe this phenomenon. The head leads and the body follows. In contrast, look at very young children; their necks are straight and their heads sit right atop their torsos where they belong.

When your head and neck are too far forward, your shoulders inevitably slouch and your chest collapses. The "shoulders back/chest up" instruction seems to make sense. But collapsed shoulders and chest result from the head and neck being out of alignment. Putting your shoulders back and your chest up does not pull your head and neck back into proper alignment. The best solution is to realign your head and neck so they are properly balanced atop your torso. This repositions your shoulders and chest properly and eliminates nervous tension.

Align Your Spine

Dancers and stage actors are taught to think of good posture as a *direction* to feel and not a *position* to hold. The direction is *upward*, starting from the top of the head. Imagine a flexible bungee chord is attached there. The bungee chord pulls gently upward. As your head pulls up, your neck straightens and lengthens. You neither lift nor tuck your chin as this gentle upward pull occurs. Your face stays on its natural plane, facing forward. When your head and neck move upward, your shoulders and chest move into proper alignment.

You can feel this sensation even while sitting down reading this book. Imagine a gentle force pulling your head upward while lengthening and straightening your neck. Stand up and try it. To find the proper place for your shoulders, raise them up toward your ears and then gently drop them back down. Do this several times to relax your shoulder muscles. You needn't lock your shoulders backward with any tension at all because your spine can carry the shoulders effortlessly. Once your head is back on top of—rather than out in front of—your torso, you will look taller and have better posture.

Your physical ritual now includes your feet, legs, breath, arms, shoulders, back, neck, and head. With your head sitting properly atop your spine, let's explore the challenge of making eye contact. Think about faces.

Your Face

People do not notice gestures because they are not looking at hands and arms. They focus instead on faces and, as they listen, most especially on eyes. Because the jury is focused on your face, you must be aware of what it is doing as you speak.

Your awareness of your face is based almost exclusively on what you see in the mirror. That reflection of your face is not really how it looks to anyone else; it is a backward mirror image of your face. The left side of your face appears to be the right side and vice versa. Perhaps this is one reason why video is so unnerving. It shows your face as it really appears with the right side on the right side; you aren't used to seeing that image. When you look in a mirror you are not conversing, arguing, or questioning. You are passively regarding your face in the mirror. That passivity may lead you to a distorted view of yourself and your natural facial animation.

One of the most frequent comments of lawyers watching themselves on video is, "I make all these weird expressions with my face!" But those expressions do not look odd to the rest of the world. The facial animation you may see as unnatural on video is what other people see all the time. This is yet another aspect of the paradox of naturalness. As with all elements of physical style, you want your face to do what it naturally does. To achieve this goal, become more aware of your own facial animation and expressions.

Your Mouth

Consider your mouth and lips. It is common for people under pressure to reveal their anxiety by tensing their lips. Some people press the lips tightly together. Others tuck one lip inside and gently chew on it. This tension looks peculiar. Instead your face should look at ease and comfortable with no visible tension, a look best described as "neutral alert." In neutral alert you appear attentive without revealing obvious emotion; you are neither smiling nor frowning. To achieve neutral alert, part your lips slightly—no more than a quarter of an inch—and breathe through both your mouth and nose. When your lips are slightly parted, they cannot tense, scowl, or tuck.

If your mouth naturally turns down in an unintended frown, be especially aware of maintaining neutral alert. Otherwise you may appear to be frowning and scowling at your own witnesses. Parting the lips slightly makes the frown disappear.

A Nervous Nose?

An experienced trial lawyer phoned Brian Johnson to discuss a mock trial he had just conducted for a big case. He was frustrated. In the discussion afterwards, one juror had commented, "I thought he looked nervous." But he hadn't felt nervous at all. "So how could she think I looked nervous?" he asked with annoyance. Luckily, there was video of his opening statement.

After watching it, Brian's advice was specific and surprising. "Watch that video again and count the number of times you touch your nose during your presentation. I counted twelve. I bet that's why she thought you looked nervous."

Sometimes your instinct to gesture can be oddly misdirected. If you inhibit your gestures, that physical energy will find an outlet. You may unconsciously touch your face repeatedly—nose, glasses, hair, etc. Because jurors are looking at your eyes and face, if your hands repeatedly rise to touch or arrange something, they will interpret that behavior as a sign of your nervousness, whether you are feeling nervous or not.

Solution: Gesture naturally, immediately, and regularly. Keep your gestural energy flowing naturally to preempt idiosyncratic distracting habits from creeping into your style.

Your Furrowed Brow

Another area of potential tension is the forehead and brow. When people concentrate, they often tense the muscles in the upper part of the face above and between the eyebrows. This furrowed brow of concentration can make you seem angry and annoyed. Use your physical ritual to become aware of what your forehead is doing. Be sure to include your face and eyes in your mnemonic ritual checklist. That way you will avoid making a scowling, negative first impression on your jury.

A furrowed brow results from tension in the forehead that draws the eyebrows together. To fix the problem, gently move the muscles in your forehead in opposite directions. When you lift your eyebrows slightly, the tension disappears. Lift your brows whenever you sense that your forehead and brows are tense. Look in a mirror to see this subtle effect. By moving your mouth and your forehead slightly, your face looks alert yet neutral—neither scowling nor artificially happy.

Eye Contact

Everyone knows that eye contact is important. It's as true of personal conversations as it is when speaking to a jury. Ultimately, credibility hinges on the answer to this question: "Can you look me in the eye as you tell me that?" If you don't look fact finders in the eye, you won't be credible.

Eye contact is also an important element of listening. When a witness is answering your questions, you need to consciously *listen with your eyes* and focus on him to make sure you hear what he is saying. If your eyes are focused on your notes while the witness speaks, you will inevitably miss something important. The brain cannot simultaneously read your notes and listen attentively to the answer.

Finally, you must focus your eyes and focus your brain to be able to think effectively on your feet. You can't focus your brain if you don't focus your eyes. This idea is developed further in the chapter about the brain, but it is useful to consider the issue as it affects your eyes.

Even though you *know* you should look people in the eye, making eye contact can be surprisingly difficult when speaking under pressure in the courtroom. There are two reasons for this difficulty. First, everyone has a personal mannerism that dictates where the eyes focus while thinking. Some people think while casting their eyes up to the ceiling; others look at the floor to think, while still others look off to the side. These mannerisms do not need to be eliminated, but they must be controlled. If your eyes flit up to the ceiling as you cast about for the next word or phrase, don't stare at the ceiling for too long. Raise your awareness of your own mannerism and control it. If your eyes break contact briefly, it's not a big problem. But if your eyes appear to linger on the ceiling, floor, or wall for too long, you will look distracted, absent-minded, or simply stumped. The secret to eye contact is to keep returning to focus on people, not things.

Follow this simple rule: never begin speaking until your eyes are focused on another person—either jurors or witnesses. When talking to a witness, don't say a word until you have lifted your eyes up and out of your notes and focused on the person on the stand. Resist the powerful temptation to begin speaking while your eyes are still focused on your notes. Talk to people, not paper.

Another factor that makes eye contact challenging is the stoic facial expressions of most jurors. In conversation you get regular subtle feedback from people. They nod, raise their eyebrows, smile, frown, and make those reassuring noises that indicate they are listening. We expect and need some type of physical and/or verbal indication that we are being listened to. Yet when speaking to a jury (or any audience for that matter), almost all of that feedback vanishes. You find yourself talking to a stony-faced group that offers few clues about what they are thinking. If a friend or colleague looked at you with such a stoical expression you would probably ask, "What's wrong? Why are they looking at me like that?"

You may find these stoic expressions intimidating and distracting, yet they are natural for jurors listening to you. It is not their job to telegraph their responses with nods, smiles, or frowns. Thankfully, some jurors may provide limited physical responses, and an advocate's eyes tend to gravitate to those people on the jury. But generally jurors sit poker-faced. They may look unfriendly, even hostile. Don't let this throw you. Your job is to make eye contact with all the jurors, no matter how difficult this sometimes may be.

Juror Number Three

When the attorney speaks to the jury in closing argument, one juror responds in the most unnerving manner. He rolls his eyes, looks down, and shakes his head back and forth. To make matters worse, he audibly exhales with a not-so-subtle snort of apparent disbelief.

The attorney, rattled by this response, whispers afterward to his client, "Juror Number Three is dead set against us. Be prepared for the worst." Following closing arguments, the jury retires to deliberate. When they return to the courtroom the attorney is stunned by the verdict—in his client's favor!

Mystified, he approaches Juror Number Three in the hallway and politely says, "Sir, may I please ask you a question? When

I spoke to the jury you responded like this," whereupon he demonstrates the headshaking, snorting behavior. The juror replies, "Oh no, man, when you were talking I was thinking, 'You don't have to convince me, buddy!'"

Helpful hint: You can't tell a book by its cover, and you can't always tell how a juror is responding to your argument based on body language. Don't give up on a juror who is looking at you funny. He might be your strongest ally during deliberations.

One reason eye contact is challenging has to do with our old friend adrenaline. In his book *Complications: A Surgeon's Notes on an Imperfect Science*, Dr. Atul Gawande writes about a scientific examination of extreme facial blushing under the pressure of performance:

> *In an odd experiment conducted a couple of years ago, two social psychologists...wired subjects with facial temperature sensors and put them on one side of a one-way mirror. The mirror was then removed to reveal an entire audience staring at them from the other side. Half the time the audience members were wearing dark glasses, and half the time, they were not. Strangely, subjects blushed only when they could see the audience's eyes.*

Psychologists studying the causes of blushing had uncovered a physiological change in the body triggered by eye contact alone. Performance pressure (speaking to audiences or juries) triggers adrenaline flow, increases blood pressure, and for some speakers, it causes intense blushing of the face and neck. It is especially apparent at the beginning of a presentation when the audience is most focused on the speaker. But these subjects were not even required to speak; they merely had to stand in silence while being stared at by all those eyes. Eye contact alone increased adrenaline flow, blood pressure, and facial temperature. When the sunglasses blocked eye contact, subjects did not blush.

Being stared at by a group triggers a predator-prey response, and the fight-or-flight response of adrenaline. This physiological response to the gaze of others may help explain why so many speakers find it difficult to sustain eye contact with listeners, even when they know they should.

Despite the physiological challenge of eye contact, you can control where you focus your eyes. Look at jurors individually and repeatedly, even those jurors with the most unresponsive expressions. Sustained eye contact will enhance your credibility with jurors, and help you concentrate on a witness' answers.

Use this simple technique to get your eyes under your control. During those few seconds of silence before you utter a word, look at the perimeter of your jury and make eye contact with the people at the four corners: front row, far right; back row, far right; back row, far left; front row, far left. Within that target area are all the eyes you want to contact. If you stake out the perimeter of your jury, you will help your brain see everyone sitting before you.

How long should you make contact? Here's an analogy for the proper duration of eye contact. Imagine you are watering a garden, and your goal is to water every plant in the garden evenly. You sweep the hose back and forth across the garden plants randomly. You don't want to soak just one plant, washing away the soil from its roots, but to water every plant equally. Similarly, when you look at the jury, look at them all regularly and consistently. You may linger on each pair of eyes for only a second or two, but you can create the feeling that you are talking to them all individually, all the time.

A discussion earlier in this chapter urged you to avoid random pacing. Pacing distracts juries and requires them to follow meaningless movement around the courtroom. But pacing also robs them of eye contact. One of the liabilities of pacing back and forth in front of the jury is that you can't make consistent eye contact with everyone. As you move to one side, the folks on the opposite side see your backside and not your eyes. When you move in the opposite direction, the other side is deprived of eye contact. So stand still most of the time and let your eyes move back and forth and up and down, randomly making eye contact.

Eyes and Notes

When you need to look at your notes, don't be afraid to stop and read. Jurors don't mind if you look at your notes occasionally, but they do mind if you talk to your notes. If you stand up and read a script word-for-word, your jury and your client will be very poorly served. (Chapter Two discusses notes in detail.) Jurors don't like to be read to, but they do expect that a trial lawyer will periodically look at notes. So when you do, don't rush. Stop and read. Look down long enough to see where you are and what you want to say next. Then bring your eyes back up, focus on a human being, and begin speaking again.

Summary

To master the challenge of controlling and coordinating your advocate body, you must cope with both your conscious and unconscious behaviors while under pressure in the courtroom. Sometimes you will deliberately jump-start instinctive behaviors such as natural gesturing. Other times your conscious brain helps to prevent unconscious behaviors, such as nervous fidgeting or pacing. Simply telling yourself to be natural will not work.

Adrenaline is a natural source of energy in the courtroom, but it can be a nuisance unless you understand and channel it. Be prepared to cope with it each time you make a presentation. Realize that adrenaline can make your legs, arms, hands, and voice tremble.

Breathe consciously, using deliberate breathing to control the volume of your voice and to calm yourself. Find and release your own natural instinct to gesture, making sure you have a technique for jump-starting your gestures at the beginning of each presentation. Pay attention to your body's alignment. Release tension in your face, and make eye contact with the judge, jury, and witnesses.

Develop a physical ritual you will use each time you go into court. Practice your physical ritual until it becomes second nature. Use the mantras on the following page to flesh out your ritual and to keep you focused on developing a reliable, persuasive technique.

Mantras of Self-Instruction

- [ ] Plant your feet and stand still.
- [ ] Pause, take a breath, and feel the floor.
- [ ] Float the knees.
- [ ] Center the hips.
- [ ] Move with a purpose.
- [ ] Breathe consciously.
- [ ] Use abdominal breathing.
- [ ] Gesture larger, longer, slower, and smoother.
- [ ] Place your hands in the ready position.
- [ ] Ready, release, and sometimes, relax.
- [ ] Jump-start your gestures with give, chop, or show.
- [ ] Fill the zone of gesture.
- [ ] Gesture "on the shelf."
- [ ] Align your spine and think: upward.
- [ ] Part your lips, unfurrow your brow.
- [ ] Talk to people, not paper.
- [ ] Find the four corners of your jury.
- [ ] Make eye contact with all your jurors.

Chapter Two

Your Brain

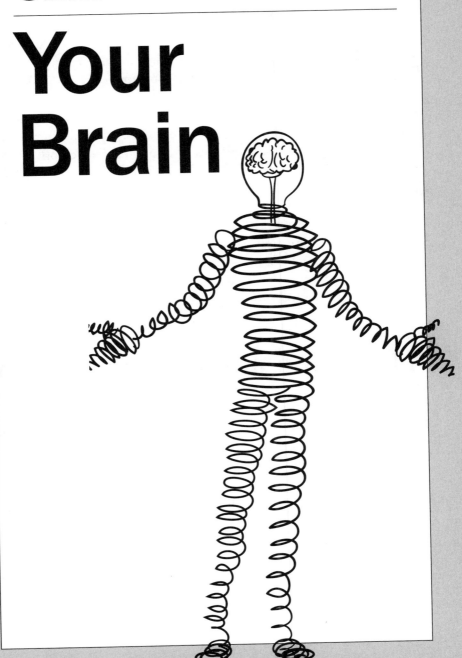

A drenaline profoundly affects your brain as well as your muscles. It is imperative that you understand the impact it has on your cognitive processes, and that you learn how to control and channel its power.

Adrenaline alters how you experience the passage of time. This can help, or hinder, your ability to function as an advocate, as well as your effectiveness in speaking clearly and persuasively under pressure. Adrenaline can be an enemy, by making you more nervous and causing you to speak too quickly, or it might befriend you, by creating the sense that you have plenty of time to contemplate what to say.

Perhaps you've noticed that most public speakers talk too quickly when they get nervous. This happens when adrenaline flows to a speaker's brain. It creates the illusion of a time warp; time seems to pass more slowly. To compensate, speakers often accelerate the pace of their speech, but talking too fast only makes thinking much more difficult for both speaker and listener. When you're under pressure, you need extra time to gather and process your thoughts.

Adrenaline and the Time Warp

Induced by a rush of adrenaline, the time warp is a vital complement to the fight-or-flight energy sent to your muscles. When threatened, you must decide whether to stand your ground and fight, or turn on your heels and flee. It would be ideal if you had lots of time to weigh your options and make the right choice when making a life-or-death decision. But you don't have the luxury of time; you must respond instantly to a perceived threat. In this moment of crisis, adrenaline helps you make the right decision by altering your perception of time's passage. It seems to expand the moment, enabling you to weigh your options and make the best choice. You may have experienced this phenomenon if you have ever genuinely feared for your life.

Consider this scenario: You are driving down the street towards an intersection. The light is green. Being a defensive driver, you glance left and then right as you approach to make certain that no vehicle is running the red. Suddenly, there it is! A big green garbage truck is barreling towards the red light, speeding right toward your driver's side door. You've got three seconds to save yourself. You think, *"I'm about to die!"*

If you have survived such a moment, you'll recall this feeling of time slowing down. Survivors' accounts of their experiences are consistent: "When I saw that garbage truck, I thought I was going to die! And everything slowed way down." They frequently add: "At that moment, my whole life flashed in front of me!" How, in three seconds, can there be time for your whole life to flash before you? That detailed historical review of your existence occurs as your brain is simultaneously weighing a number of complex alternatives:

Swerve left? No, oncoming traffic!
Swerve right? No, little kids on the sidewalk!
Slam on the brakes? Too late for that!
Speed up? Yes, floor it!

Although scientists cannot fully explain how the time warp works, it's thanks to adrenaline that the brain seemingly has extra time to perform all those complex calculations (involving speed, mass, distance, and even ethics) necessary to assure your safety.

The human experience of time is highly subjective. In everyday life, time appears to pass much faster or slower depending on your circumstances. When you're having a good time, time seems to fly by. If you're bored and watching the clock, time slows to a crawl. Of course, the actual passage of time never really changes: a second lasts one second, a minute lasts one minute, an hour takes an hour.

Your subjective experience of time's passage, whether faster or slower, is also influenced by how much information your brain is processing in any given moment. During an adrenaline rush, as you instantly analyze and respond to a perceived threat, your brain processes information at an unusually high rate. In his classic book *On the Experience of Time*, Robert E. Ornstein refers to studies that found "…the amount of mental content in an interval determines its subjective duration." In other words, if your brain is processing increased amounts of information, as it must in a life-or-death situation (or in a jury trial), you may subjectively experience time as slowing down.

Another theory involves heart rate and adrenaline. Ornstein refers to a study that showed "...with more 'beats' in an interval, time experience lengthens." Your resting heart rate is about 60 beats per minute. The regular rhythmic tempo of everyday life is *one heartbeat = one second*. Under the influence of adrenaline, however, your heart rate accelerates dramatically to 120 beats per minute or more. Your brain registers twice as many heartbeats per minute, and therefore twice as many "seconds" appear to pass in a given interval. Paradoxically, time seems to slow down as your heart rate speeds up. Does a doubling of your heart rate make time seem to pass twice as slowly? Time perception is probably too idiosyncratic to permit a general answer.

In the courtroom, you can turn the subjectivity of time's passing to your advantage. Make it part of your technique; train yourself to channel and exploit the time warp. Rather than allowing it to prompt you to speak faster, use the time warp to give yourself the sense that you have more time to think. Instead of your whole life passing before you, now all available thoughts and words will flash in front of you.

Seeking the Zone of Concentration

Being "pumped," as athletes are in competition, involves both muscles and mind. Muscles are highly energized, the mind sharply focused. Athletes who learn to exploit the benefits of the time warp refer to this heightened state of concentration as being "in the zone." While in this zone of concentration, an athlete has more time to make decisions concerning the right moves to execute in order to play the game successfully. The great home run slugger Ted Williams famously exploited the time warp in the batter's box, though he insisted he was just waiting for "a good ball to hit." Being in the zone of concentration allowed him plenty of time to decide whether, and how, to swing at a pitch.

For an advocate experiencing the time warp, silence can be particularly uncomfortable and intimidating. Time appears to pass so slowly that a silence of almost any length seems oppressively long, especially at the beginning of a presentation, when the initial adrenaline rush is most intense.

To compensate for these "long" silences, nervous advocates often rush to fill the void with thinking noises—*uh* and *um*—and they talk too fast. This sets a tempo that is impossible to sustain. Talking fast may fill the silence, but it also eliminates your thinking time. As a result, your brain cannot formulate clear, concise sentences or questions. Even if you could speak articulately at a fast pace, jurors, witnesses, and court reporters couldn't keep up with you. Although your words might be understood, their meaning is not. For the listener, words spoken too quickly go in one ear and out the other. You cannot be persuasive when your tongue races. Moments of silence are a gift of adrenaline's time warp. Use them.

How Many Seconds in a Pause?

During video review at a trial skills training program, a lawyer comes to watch the playback of her opening statement. "My performance was terrible!" she blurts out to the instructor. "I couldn't think of what to say next. The pauses were endless."

During the playback, the patient instructor quantifies those seemingly endless pauses by counting aloud: "one-thousand-one, one-thousand-two, one-thousand-three." To the advocate's amazement, most of her so-called "pauses" last only one second, a couple of them for two seconds. Just one "pause" lasts for three whole seconds!

Existing in the time warp, this attorney's highly subjective sense of time led her to believe, mistakenly, that her opening statement had been undermined by supposedly lengthy pauses—pauses that, to the listener, didn't even exist. By the end of the video she is flabbergasted: "That is so weird. While I was standing there, the pauses appeared to be soooo long. But now I hear that they weren't long at all. A silence of only two or three seconds doesn't even count as a pause."

Helpful hint: For jurors listening and existing in real time rather than in the time warp, three seconds last a mere three seconds. To them, three seconds don't even register as a pause, much less a problem.

As it does for athletes in the almost magical zone of concentration, adrenaline's time warp can work for you instead of against you. When you exploit the time warp, your silences will still feel much longer than normal—but in a good and useful way. With practice, the time warp will afford you what feels like an extra long interval to consider what you want to say. Those three seconds of silence feel like twelve. What a luxury to have so much apparent time to think! You've got all the time in the world to choose the right word or formulate your next sentence. You can weigh the merits of ending a line of questioning or delving more deeply into a topic. You've got all the time necessary to choose your next word, respond to an objection, or compose your next question. Silence becomes a valuable tool, an important part of your technique.

Take conscious control of the silence in the courtroom *before* you start to speak. When you first stand up, don't say anything. Pause for a few seconds, and count silently to yourself: one-thousand-one, one-thousand-two, one-thousand-three. It will seem like a long time, but it isn't. Purposefully focus on hearing the silence in the room. Once you've heard it, use it when you speak. Weave short, one-second gaps into your delivery. Say a phrase and stop (silence); say another phrase and stop (silence). At the end of a sentence, and especially at the end of a topic or line of questioning, pause even longer and listen. During that silence—think! You will find that once you begin to focus on silence and its intersection with speech, you grow comfortable using it.

Exploiting the time warp and its partner, silence, enhances your capacity to think and speak effectively. It also increases the jury's capacity to understand and be persuaded by what you have to say. Silence is a critical component of your jurors' thought process. They need time to think. If you want to persuade people, you need to give them time to reflect. Jurors aren't persuaded by what you say *as* you are saying it; they are persuaded when they have a moment in silence to think about what you just said.

Consider the thought process of your jurors. They are not trained, as you are, to think like a lawyer. One of the challenges of being a juror is to get comfortable with legal issues, legal jargon, and legal concepts. It's foreign territory, cognitively speaking. Jurors need more time than you do to think through what is being said—to grasp your meaning fully, and ultimately to be persuaded. It is only *after* you have spoken that the jury has time to consider your words. The amount of time you require to choose your words is certainly less than the amount of time your jurors need to think about what you've just said. Give them time to think and process, and then form an opinion.

Echoic Memory

In the courtroom, jurors use "echoic memory." As the word "echo" implies, that is literally what happens in the brain of an attentive listener…

> As you speak… *As you speak…*
> the juror's brain… *the juror's brain…*
> echoes back what you say… *echoes back what you say.*

Echoic memory is used routinely in everyday life. For example, if you hear a phone number, you may simply say it aloud as a memory aid—*555-1212… 555-1212… 555-1212*—until you grab a pencil to write it down. That repetition or echoing helps the brain remember.

During an examination, the echoic memory in a juror's brain might be represented as such:

Q: What do you do for a living?
A: I'm a rocket scientist.
Juror: *(Oh, he's a rocket scientist.)*

Students taking notes while listening to a professor's lecture are engaged in a version of echoic memory. They echo into their laptops or their notebooks the important ideas the professor says. If he speaks too quickly, however, the students are unable to take notes effectively. Whether the listeners are students taking notes or jurors simply taking note of what you are saying, they need time to let your thoughts sink in. The more complex and/or important the information you give your jury, the more time they need to echo it back in their own minds in order to grasp it and be persuaded. When you give your jurors time to think about what you say, you are exploiting *persuasive silence*.

Silence is Golden

At a National Institute for Trial Advocacy training program a seasoned attorney serving on the faculty is demonstrating closing argument. His delivery is exceptional, and his use of pauses—those persuasive silences—is especially noteworthy. Afterward, a participant exclaimed, "Now I understand how effective silence and pausing can be, especially during a closing. His pauses gave us so much time to think about, and be persuaded by, his arguments."

When another faculty member repeats these compliments to him, he chuckles and confesses, "That's so funny. I was actually struggling to remember what I wanted to say next. So those pauses were not intentional; they seemed really long to me while I was searching my brain for the next thought!"

Helpful hint: Because of the time warp, silence of any duration feels longer to the speaker than it is to the listener. Use that silence to think about what's next, and give your jurors a chance to process what you've just said.

Thinking On Your Feet

Once you realize that you need time (and silence) to think on your feet, the next step is to understand exactly *how* to think on your feet. Should you read? What about memorization? Can you write out what you want to say? What's so bad about simply reading or reciting everything?

Do Not Read

Do not read to the jury from your notes during opening and closing. Reading is deadly. You may be tempted to do so, thinking that it will increase the chance that your delivery will be perfect. But the only perfection you will achieve is to be perfectly boring! It is unlikely that you have been trained, as broadcasters and actors are, to read aloud skillfully. Reading aloud is an art unto itself, and many actors can't even do it well. (Ever watch the Academy Awards? Some film actors can't read a few lines off a monitor!)

Everyone makes the same cognitive mistakes when reading aloud. You read too fast. You read without natural expression and inflection, burying your nose in your notes. If you decide to read in the courtroom, you will rarely look fact finders in the eye, and you will lack credibility. You will sound and look like you are reading—because you are! Listeners are not fooled by reading. If you wish to persuade people, you mustn't read *at* them, you must talk *to* them.

During examinations, resist the temptation to read from your notes as you ask questions. You do not possess the gift of prophecy. While preparing for a trial, you cannot predict what a witness will say. This is true even during direct examination with a well-prepared witness. People are unpredictable, especially when performing under pressure and feeling nervous. Reading a list of written questions presupposes that you know the exact words the witness will use to answer each question. Here is an example of what can happen if advocates bury their eyes in notes and simply read the questions. The advocate wasn't listening, and didn't expect the second part of each answer:

Q: Ms. Hernandez, tell us where you live.
A: I live in San Diego with my husband.
Q: Are you married?
A: Yes, with two kids.
Q: Do you have any children?
A: Yes, a boy 6 and a girl 8.
Q: What are their ages?

As silly as that sounds, it is a common and comic occurrence at trial advocacy training programs. The advocate incorrectly assumes that the witness will give precisely the answer imagined. The extra detail provided with each answer was not anticipated. The problem is compounded when advocates are so focused on reading the next question from a legal pad that they don't listen to the answers given by the witness. The result is absurd.

Do Not Recite

Recitation—repeating aloud or declaiming a text from memory—is a highly specialized skill. Even with years of training and practice, professional actors in a stage play require weeks of rehearsal to memorize and recite their lines accurately and confidently. As a busy lawyer, you can't spend weeks memorizing your courtroom presentations. You're apt to have a memory slip—and a single slip can undermine your confidence. If you can't think of the next word to say, you're stumped. If a critical issue arises after you have painstakingly memorized your opening, it will be challenging to incorporate new facts smoothly. Memorization *sounds* wrong to listeners. You look a bit glassy-eyed when reciting, since your mind is elsewhere: on the task of memorizing what you wrote. So don't try to memorize and recite your courtroom presentations; the risk of error is great.

Since you're not going to read and you're not going to recite, you have only one option left. Talk.

Structured Improvisation

The style of thinking you do on your feet in the courtroom is best described as structured improvisation. In advance, you structure carefully the order of topics you intend to talk about in your opening statement or closing argument; then, you improvise word-by-word, just as you do in conversational speech. Your brain is quite adept at this kind of thinking and speaking.

Suppose you say to a colleague, "We need to talk about the meeting yesterday and the seminar tomorrow." Here is your structure:

1) meeting
2) seminar

Using that two-part structure, you simply talk, improvising the words as you go along. In the courtroom you structure longer presentations with more information, but as you already have experience with that skill, you do it naturally.

Think about a story from your own life that you have told numerous times—a personal anecdote about something humorous, frightening, or bizarre. If you were asked to tell a listener about that experience, you wouldn't hesitate or struggle, because you lived the story and have told it—in effect, have practiced telling it—many times before. Now imagine that you were asked to tell that same anecdote again to a different listener, immediately, but with one additional, impossible requirement: you must tell it verbatim, word-for-word, exactly as you did the first time.

You couldn't do that. Nobody could. This would not indicate that suddenly you were unable to remember the event. It simply would mean that you could not remember and repeat verbatim the words you used to describe it, although you had uttered that description just minutes before. If you cannot accomplish this task even with a familiar anecdote, you can hardly hope to deliver an opening statement or closing argument that you wrote in the recent past. The brain isn't built that way.

Telling your personal story requires a form of structured improvisation. The sequence of events is the structure; you improvise around it, retelling the anecdote using different words, phrases, and sentences. Structured improvisation also works for examinations. Plan your examinations according to the topic areas you wish to discuss, and then improvise your questions around that structure while listening carefully to the answers you receive.

Speaking in court using structured improvisation is like performing a kind of verbal jazz. You can learn to be comfortable living in this cognitive state, poised between the opposites of well-planned structure and free-form improvisation. You have to prepare carefully for what you hope and expect will happen in court. But once you are making an opening statement or examining a witness, you need to deal with what is really happening, which may be different from what you expected. In essence, you train your brain to structure and remember your ideas in a specific order, but not with the precise words you actually will use.

Athletes playing a team sport, like football, practice the plays they intend to use in a game. Once the game begins, however, the players must improvise if the quarterback fumbles the ball, or the passing play is broken up by the blitzing linebacker, or the pass receiver slips and falls. Trial advocacy might be described as a verbal game in which similarly unexpected things can and do occur. Just as in a game, there are opposing teams, a judge acting as referee, definite rules governing how the game must be played, and a winner and a loser. The game of advocacy is played—as are the games of tennis, volleyball or handball—in a confined space called a court. As with any athletic competition, this verbal battle of wits requires practice and preparation, as well as the ability to improvise, deal with the unexpected, and go with the flow during the game.

Do Not Read and Talk Simultaneously

Your brain is not experienced at talking and reading simultaneously. In everyday life, when you talk, you talk, and when you read, you read. Do not create notes with prose paragraphs that must be read. Such notes are a trap. The more words you write on your legal pad, the less helpful the notes become. When you are talking in court, there just isn't time to read all those words. If you stand up in court with a lengthy, detailed script, the temptation to read it will be irresistible. Your brain doesn't naturally talk and read at the same time, so it must do one or the other. It chooses reading, because that is the safer choice. But reading inevitably is boring and unpersuasive.

The written word is processed in a different part of the brain than the spoken word. Functional magnetic resonance imaging, or fMRI, which can "look" into the thinking brain, reveals that reading and speaking happen in two different areas. To attempt to read your notes while talking at the same time is analogous to running two incompatible software programs on your computer. Your brain's cognitive hard drive will crash, just as the computer will. So pick the proper cognitive software: talk to your jury and witnesses. Reading aloud isn't persuasive, talking is. And it is what you already do whenever you communicate.

In dissuading you from reading in court, we don't mean to suggest that you can't have notes to guide your structured improvisation. Jurors expect that a lawyer will look at a legal pad periodically. It's perfectly okay to look at your notes, just don't *talk* to your notes. There's a huge difference, and it's all a matter of timing. The secret of creating useful notes is to conceive of them as a private visual aid.

Notes as Your Visual Aid

Notes are very often a necessity. In a complex case, notes lying on a lectern or counsel table guide you through your speeches or examinations. They help you structure and remember what you want to say, and are a comforting security blanket when your mind goes blank.

Truly useful speaking notes serve as visual aids. Fundamentally they differ in purpose and design from the "thinking notes" you jot down initially as you collect your thoughts about a case, and are distinct from the "listening notes" you write on your legal pad as opposing counsel examines a witness. Additionally, those thinking and listening notes are not big enough—and often not legible enough—to be a good visual aid.

Good visual aids provide a structure around which a speaker can improvise. Here are some rules to help you create good notes for use in the courtroom.

Write big. Use a pen that makes a fat line on the paper. Big, thick writing can be seen easily, even at a distance. Notes written too small are indecipherable lying on counsel table three or four feet away. Consider the distance your eyes are from the page that you are reading. If your notes are lying on a lectern twice the distance from your eyes, shouldn't they be written twice as big? If they are lying on counsel table three times the distance from your eyes, shouldn't they be written at least three times as large as regular writing? If you create notes using your computer, double or triple the size of the font, from 10- or 12-point to 24- or 26-point. Make big notes that are easy to read, so when you glance at them, the words leap off the page. You'll be amazed at how much easier it is to speak with notes you can read easily. They should look something like this:

Write big.

Write legibly.

Keep notes simple.

Keep notes handy.

Write legibly. Carefully print your notes so that they are legible. It takes a bit more time and effort, but it's well worth it. Key words, dates, or dollar amounts should be printed in red to highlight their importance; emphasize important words with a yellow highlighter. When you write legibly as well as large, it prevents you from putting too many words on a page. That's a good thing, because it reinforces the next rule.

Keep notes simple. Less is more. Fewer words are more useful. Boil down your big ideas to just a few words that will trigger the whole thought. Remember, the more words you put on paper, the less useful the notes become. Avoid prose sentences. Write down the structure of your ideas, then improvise around that structure. Don't waste space writing, "Good morning, members of the jury, my name is…"

Keep notes handy. Place your notes where you can see them easily. If you are required to speak from behind a lectern, step back about twelve inches—reading your notes should require only a downward shift of your eyes. If you step to the side of the lectern, position yourself so that you can see your notes without moving your feet. Beware of the tendency to step to the side of the lectern, and then forward a step or two. That makes it impossible to read your notes without crab-walking backward to glance at them. Stand *still* where you can see your notes, especially if you need to look at them often.

Practice using your notes. Get on your feet and talk out loud while using the notes. Speaking with notes is a skill that must be practiced. There is nothing particularly natural about glancing at notes while speaking and making regular eye contact with jurors or witnesses. Work on it.

Read when you need to. If you need to look carefully at your notes to orient yourself, simply say, "Let's move on." That generic transition line justifies returning to your notes to see what's next in the structure. When you look at the notes, take your time. Fact finders know what you are doing, and they aren't bothered by it. They're thinking about what you just said, or the question and answer they just heard during examination. Jurors don't mind interruptions. Looking at your notes offers them a kind of break, resembling a commercial on TV or radio ("And now a word from our sponsor…"). Once you finish looking at your notes, return to your regularly scheduled opening statement. Once again, look the jurors in their eyes and speak directly to them. If you do, they'll be patient when you consult your notes.

When you look, *really* look at your notes and read what is written there. Glance backward at the previous topic you just covered. If you forgot to mention something, fix the problem by saying, "Members of the jury, I neglected to mention something important about that last topic." In this way, you turn the lemon of forgetting into the lemon-ade of "something important." Jurors will pay close attention when you tell them it's important. No harm is done. One reason advocates are so glued to their notes is that they are petrified at the prospect of forgetting something important. You needn't be afraid of forgetting. Give yourself time to look over your notes and make sure you have covered everything important in the previous topic before moving on to the next.

Plan to Forget

Many advocates bury their noses in their notes because they're gripped by the fear, "What if I forget?" But that's the wrong question! The proper question to ask and answer is, "*When* I forget, how will I re-cover?" That you will forget periodically while speaking under pressure is a given. Think how easily you can lose your train of thought in casual conversation. You pause and confess, "I lost my train of thought. What was I talking about?" If this happens regularly during casual conversa-tion, it's bound to happen in the courtroom. The obvious solution? Plan to forget. Know that it is going to happen, and be prepared for when it does.

As we have suggested, the transitional utterance "Let's move on" can be a useful way to explain and justify your taking a look at your notes and pausing to gather your thoughts. You are moving on, so it makes sense to refer to your notes to see what is next. Or, you can use the same line simply to stop and think. The jury will understand what you are doing. You have announced that you are moving on, and the jury sees that you are thinking. This is a moment when it is particularly important that you are comfortable with silence. Trust that the jury is watching your cognitive wheels turn. Take the time you need to think about what should come next.

If you are between topics and cannot remember your next area of discussion, simply say aloud the question that is in the forefront of your mind: "What's next?" Having asked that question, look at your notes and find the answer. This is a common storytelling device, especially when telling a story to children:

> Then Goldilocks knocked on the door. What happened next, boys and girls? The door slowly swung open.

You can use this same device in your opening statement when narrating what happened.

> Then they signed the contract on October 28th. What happened next? On November 3rd the plaintiff...

But what if you can't remember a precise fact, such as a date or dollar amount? One way to deal with that problem is to say,

> Now the date the contract was signed [*you suddenly can't remember, so you say*]...

> I want to get this exactly right [*and return to consult your notes*]...

> the date was November 3rd.

As you say, "I want to get this exactly right," look purposefully at your notes and check the fact to get it right. The jury sees such careful behavior as an indication of due diligence; it can even boost the speaker's credibility.

Label Your Problem

Sometimes thinking on your feet means you will get lost or confused about where you are in your structure. A talented trial lawyer admits that he has a tendency to go off on a tangent, especially during closing argument. When he finds himself straying from his main point, he labels his problem and says, "Members of the jury, I've clearly gone off on a tangent here. Please forgive me, and let me return to my main point."

With that simple course correction, he acknowledges his problem, and fixes it. He has made a frank confession of his humanity and fallibility. It is a breath of fresh air for the jury.

Label your problem: The jury will respect you for your forthright honesty.

Before you try any of these techniques in the courtroom, pause long enough in silence to make sure you really can't remember what you wished to say. The next thought may not quite be on the tip of your tongue, but it is almost certainly somewhere in your brain. Give yourself a moment to find it. Be aware that it is at such moments that the time warp is most oppressive. Don't panic. Take your time. See if the thought is somewhere in your head. Take a breath, open your hands, and give yourself a moment of silence. If the thought doesn't materialize, act on your plan to forget and use one of the techniques suggested above. If you practice saying these "Plan to Forget" parachute lines before you need them, you will be ready to use them when the moment comes. Say them aloud right now to begin that process:

Let's move on.
What's next?
What happened next?
I want to get this exactly right.
Excuse me, but I've lost my train of thought.

Scripting as a Preliminary Step

Some advocates find it absolutely essential to write out their courtroom presentations before creating the final version of their notes. If writing feels like a necessary part of your preparation, don't fight it. But do recognize that writing is only an interim step in the process, not the final one. You do not write in the same style in which you speak. In law school you were trained to write like a lawyer, not conversationally. What you write is not an ideal, finished product. Even if you had a perfect photographic memory and could stand confidently and recite accurately every word you had written, it wouldn't sound natural. The stylistic elevation of legalese would sound too literary and artificial. Given this inevitable stylistic difference, writing can be a trap. For instance, in conversation you would ask, "Where do you work?" or "Where do you live?" Lawyers tend to write, "Where are you so employed?" and "Where do you so reside?" No one really speaks like that. A stilted style, loaded with legalese, will be much less persuasive to the jury.

If writing out your speech or examination helps you organize your thoughts, do it. But then reduce that writing to an outline form or bullet points. Once you've got a structure on paper, stand up and practice improvising with that structure.

Avoid Thinking Backward

It cannot be emphasized strongly enough that you should *not* try to recite in order to replicate what you wrote word-for-word. If you attempt this, you will find yourself "thinking backward." Your brain cannot simultaneously think backward to what you wrote and forward to what you are trying to say. Your thought process will crash. Your written presentation is merely one version of your product, and probably not the best version. When you say it aloud the first time, you will use the same structure, but different words to convey it. When you practice it again, yet another set of words will emerge to embody that same structure. Think forward. Describe your ideas with newly-minted sentences that will be different each time. The structure remains the same, even as the exact words change. Every time you practice, you will improve by sounding more spontaneous and more persuasive. To understand how thinking forward can help keep your train of thought on track, consider a concept from cognitive psychology.

Chunking

The human brain prefers to receive information in chunks. Chunks are batches or bites, if you will, of information. If there are many things to be remembered, the brain prefers those many bits of information to be aggregated into chunks so that there are fewer things to remember. Your ten digit phone number is a good example of this. Because ten numbers are hard to remember, your phone number is divided into three chunks: (area code) prefix - suffix. The parentheses and the dash visually break those ten numbers in three easier-to-remember chunks. Conversely, the brain also prefers that large, complex concepts be broken up into smaller, more manageable chunks. For example, when you're questioning an accident victim on direct examination, the information might be chunked in this way:

1) personal information
2) educational background
3) work experience
4) day of the accident

Your notes show the important topics (or chunks) that you will talk about in court. One way to help your listeners follow your structure is to indicate clearly when a topic or chunk is ending or beginning. The key elements here are primacy and recency. The brain is more attentive when topics start and stop—at beginnings and endings. People tend to remember the things said first (primacy) as well as the information last provided on a particular topic (recency). Chunking can refer to the macro-level structure of big topics and concepts, but it is also a useful concept for understanding the micro-level of sentence structure. The technique in the next chapter, Your Voice, will build upon this structure.

Structure:
Primacy and Recency

Listeners pay close attention to the beginnings and endings of presentations; minds often wander in the middle. The effects of primacy and recency can be plotted on a graph like the one below. Memory retention is represented by the vertical axis (left). The horizontal axis indicates passage of time (left to right). At first (A), listeners are attentive; they pay close attention at the beginning, and remember what is said. As time passes, however, attention wanes, so retention and memory drop. When the listener gets a signal that the end (Z) is near—"In conclusion, members of the jury…" or "One final question, Ms. Lovejoy…"—attention once again increases and retention is higher.

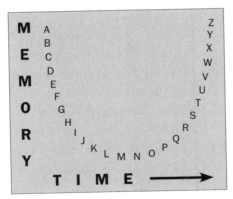

One reason people listen well at the beginning of presentations is to decide whether it's worthwhile to continue to pay close attention. You have a small window of opportunity to capture your listeners' interest. If you seize it at the beginning, it's easier to hold. You must be stylistically and substantively compelling right from the start. If you don't care about what you're saying, why should jurors?

Each new beginning is an important opportunity. Don't squander it by starting with meaningless filler such as: "This is a simple case… (*unlikely or you would have settled*); "I've just got a couple questions…" (*never true*); "How are you today, Mr. Farrell?" (*you don't really care*);

"Members of the jury, opposing counsel just told you a lot of facts" (*a pointless observation*). Whenever possible, say something at the beginning that you want the jury to remember, such as: "Isn't it true that you were text messaging when your SUV struck Ms. Hennessey?" What juror isn't going to pay attention to what follows that question? Granted, it is not always possible to start with such an obvious "grabber." In that case, you have to *sound* interesting immediately and be interested yourself. Always begin with an energy and enthusiasm that suggests you are taking the listener somewhere intriguing. When you can't capture their attention substantively, you can always grab it with the style of your delivery.

It will be easier to hold your jurors' attention in the middle if you have grabbed it at the beginning. As the words themselves imply, to *grab* and to *hold* attention takes energy—vocal and physical energy. As a speaker you must work hard immediately. You cannot afford to warm up slowly and gradually become dynamic, enthusiastic, and interesting several minutes later. If you do that, by the time you've warmed up and achieved a certain level of skill, the listener's mind will have wandered off.

Even if you begin in a way that immediately captivates the listeners, it is important to recognize that no one listens attentively 100% of the time. Minds wander. Attention fades in and out; as a result, retention rises and falls. Knowing this, your goal as an advocate is to regularly recapture those wandering, inattentive minds in the jury box and invite them to pay attention once again.

Since beginnings and endings are good, create more of them. Rather than conceive your presentation as having only one beginning and one ending, clearly delineate each topic area. Begin each new topic with a headline (primacy) and explicitly mark the conclusion of the topic (recency). If topic A of your direct examination is your witness' *educational background*, announce that topic before you begin the line of questions: "Ms. Bittova, let's focus on your educational background," marking the moment of primacy. Before moving on to the next topic, *professional experience*, close out topic A. "We've discussed your educational background, so now let's talk about your professional experience." A cross examiner might headline this way: "We've dis-

cussed who was responsible for maintaining the furnace, now let's talk
about the required annual inspections." In an opening or closing in a
criminal case, a prosecutor creates endings and beginnings by saying,
"Members of the jury, I described the charges the state must prove,
now let's examine the evidence that proves those charges." When topic
areas are demarcated in this fashion, your presentation will have many
beginnings and endings. Each time a new topic is headlined and closed
out, the daydreaming listener is invited to pay attention once again.

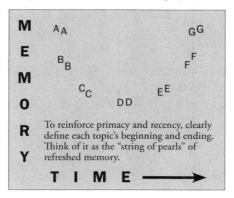

Exploiting the laws of primacy and recency will help you remember the structure of your presentation. Once you have stated aloud to
the jury the topic area you are discussing, you will discover it is easier
to focus your own thoughts, as well as your jurors', on that one subject.
It will assist your memory if you practice saying aloud just the headlines that begin and end topic areas. Once you can make connections
between these areas, then you have the structure clear in your mind.

Jesse (The Body) Ventura

Initially skeptical of the idea of primacy and recency, Brian
Johnson conducted an experiment. For one year, he began
his presentation at trial advocacy programs with the exact same
sentences. The first thing he said was: "The house in which

I live lies exactly halfway between the Equator and the North Pole. The 45th parallel runs right through my neighborhood in St. Paul, Minnesota." What did that have to do with persuasive style?

At the time the governor of Minnesota was an eccentric former professional wrestler named Jesse (The Body) Ventura. After the initial geographic reference to Minnesota, Brian referred to his governor, and offered him as an extreme example of persuasive personal style.

The experiment proved the power of primacy. Years later, people still jokingly ask him, "Do you still live halfway between the Equator and the North Pole?" That fact didn't have anything to do with advocacy or communication or persuasion! It stuck with people because it was first.

Remember: Exploit the power of primacy!

Attitude as a Tactical Choice

Attitude is a tactical choice in the courtroom. It is also a cognitive issue. Because attitude so often is sparked by emotion—you must allow your logical brain to override any inappropriate emotions with a rational point of view.

What attitude do you want to adopt when making an opening or closing, or when speaking to your witness? Your point of view will be reflected in your demeanor, inflections, and tone of voice. Why not be friendly when talking with your own witnesses? If you want the jury to like your witnesses and find them credible, talk to them as if you like them and find them credible. Unless there is good reason not to, speak to your witnesses with the socially engaging energy you use when talking to your friends and colleagues. Occasionally you may have a strategic reason to put some emotional distance between yourself and your witness, but that happens rarely. Most of the time your attitude should be friendly, polite, curious, and interested in what your witness has to say on direct.

If the issues in a specific case are very serious (involving catastrophic injury or death, for example) and the general mood is somber, make the suitable attitude choice. Attitude is a subtle and mysterious part of persuasion, and shouldn't be left to chance. On cross-examination, you may want to start out respectfully, and wait to see if the witness needs to be controlled.

Whatever you decide, make sure you can name your attitude. If you do not name it specifically, you run the risk of defaulting to something generalized, which could leave your witness and the fact finder confused about your intention. To get you started, here is a list of attitudes. Add to it as you think about tactics and strategy.

angry	disappointed	outraged
betrayed	disrespectful	parental
compassionate	emphatic	pejorative
condescending	excited	sarcastic
contemptuous	friendly	snooty
cynical	happy	surprised
defensive	hopeful	sympathetic
defeated	incredulous	understanding
deflated	optimistic	

Summary

To think on your feet under pressure, you must understand and ultimately exploit the time warp, a phenomenon created by adrenaline that makes time appear to slow down. When living in the time warp, take your time rather than speak too quickly. Embrace your altered perception and make silence a conscious part of your technique. To get into the zone of concentration, listen to the silence before you speak, then integrate that silence into your presentation, pausing briefly between phrases and sentences to think, "What's next?" This gives your jury a few moments to think about what you just said. Persuasion happens in the silence, so use it to give jurors time for their echoic memory to process your words.

Don't read or recite from memory; get comfortable with structured improvisation. Create notes that help structure your presentation and can serve as a visual aid. Write big, legibly, simply. Practice using your notes. Plan to forget; it's going to happen, so prepare for it by saying:

Let's move on.
What happened next?
I want to get this right.
Excuse me, but I've lost my train of thought.

If you need to write out your speeches or examinations as a preliminary step, do! Then reduce your structure to a simple outline or bullet points. Don't try to think backward to what you wrote; think forward to what you're trying to say next.

Focus on creating more primacy and recency in your presentations; use clearly delineated beginnings and endings as topic areas. Think and speak in phrases or chunks. Silence is punctuation made audible.

Use the mantras on the following page to hone your cognitive skills for courtroom speaking.

Mantras of Self-Instruction

- ☐ Get comfortable with the time warp.
- ☐ Enter the zone of the time warp.
- ☐ Exploit persuasive silence.
- ☐ Reading is boring.
- ☐ You do not possess the gift of prophecy.
- ☐ Do not try to recite from memory.
- ☐ Talk: Use structured improvisation.
- ☐ Don't try to read and talk simultaneously.
- ☐ Notes are your visual aid.
- ☐ Plan to forget: use parachute lines.
- ☐ Think forward, not backwards.
- ☐ Find flow and go with it.
- ☐ Exploit primacy and recency.
- ☐ Use attitude as a tactical choice.
- ☐ Think and speak in phrases (chunking).

CHAPTER THREE

Your Voice

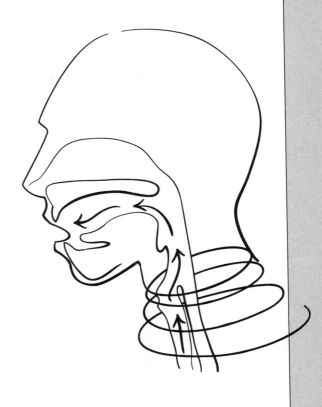

n everyday conversation, how do you use your voice expressively? How do you adjust your pace, volume, energy, pitch, and tone when talking to different people about various topics?

To speak more persuasively as an advocate, begin by listening to your own voice outside the courtroom. You may not be aware of it, but in order to communicate better we all continually make adjustments in our speech. Just as the use of natural gestures in the courtroom requires that you ask "What do I do with my hands in conversation?," now ask a similar question about your voice: "What do I do with my voice naturally and expressively when talking with friends and colleagues?" You certainly pay attention to *what* you say in conversation; now pay closer attention to *how* you say it.

Listening to Yourself

Your goal as an articulate advocate is to push beyond what you do naturally with your voice. You need a technique that will give you the vocal power and stamina to speak in court with persuasive expressivity for extended periods of time. If you are soft-spoken, you must get comfortable with speaking consistently at a greater volume. If you are shy and introverted, you need to learn how to transcend those tendencies and become a zealous advocate for your client's cause. If you talk very fast, you must be able to slow down and control your pace. Most important, you should be reliably fluent and articulate every time the judge looks at you and says: "Counsel, you may proceed."

Another challenge is to evaluate your own voice objectively during recorded video playback. When you hear your voice played back through a television in a video review of a courtroom performance, on voice mail, or an answering machine, you probably sound rather odd—at least to yourself. It's important that you get past this hypercritical, subjective response, as it's unlikely that you sound funny or peculiar to anyone else.

Improving your voice begins with a clear-eyed assessment of its current state. To evaluate your voice accurately, it helps to understand why it sounds funny to you on a recording. The answer involves two different ways we hear ourselves speak. When your vocal cords vibrate, those vibrations travel both through the air (to a listener's eardrums or to your own) as well as through your body. You can observe this phenomenon by gently putting your index fingers in both ears and speaking a few words. Recite the beginning of the *Gettysburg Address* or the *Pledge of Allegiance*. Your fingers block the vibrations that normally travel through the air to reach your eardrums. What you hear instead are additional vibrations traveling through the flesh and bone of your neck and skull to your inner ears. Now remove your fingers from your ears, and place the palm of one hand on your upper chest right below your neck. Say a few words, and notice that as you speak your upper torso also vibrates, which you can feel in your upper chest. This seems particularly intense because your body itself is vibrating, not just the air near your ears.

Without these lower-pitched vibrations conducted by flesh and bone, our own voices often sound "nasal" to us. There's nothing wrong with your voice, however! Begin to use it in the courtroom with greater power, confidence, expressivity, and authority. Abandon your self-critical response and tackle the real challenge: using your voice more persuasively.

Your Lungs and Diaphragm

Chapter One discussed the necessity and mechanics of breathing consciously. This not only calms you down, it allows more oxygen to reach your brain and enables you to speak with greater power, projection, and control. The muscles that govern respiration include the diaphragm and the intercostal muscles between your ribs. All of these should be warmed up before you begin speaking in court.

Observe your breathing as you read this paragraph:

Your autonomic nervous system controls your breath. A small, subtle movement is taking place in your lower torso. Now begin to breathe consciously, and inhale more deeply. Did you notice how much more completely and efficiently you breathed when you fully inflated your lungs? Take an even longer, deeper breath. Work the muscles of respiration more vigorously; push against your belt.

Intercostal Muscles and Your Ribcage

The ability to consciously control your breath is the foundation of mastering your voice. In addition to the diaphragm, the intercostal muscles between your ribs help the lungs expand. Place your hands on the bottom of your ribcage, at the sides of your body about halfway between your waist and armpits. Take a deep breath, and feel the outward movement of the intercostal muscles as your lungs expand. Breathing consciously and deeply creates a three-dimensional expansion: your abdomen moves forward, your ribs push out at the side, and your back extends to the rear.

Vocal Fatigue

A long day of speaking in the courtroom can cause vocal fatigue. It's important to understand that the solution for a tired voice lies not in your larynx but in your abdomen. Your voice tires from a lack of breath support. If not enough air is passing over your vocal cords, you may add stress and tension to your throat as you attempt to project. This makes your voice tired and eventually hoarse.

If you feel your voice getting tired, focus on your breath support. Work the abdominal muscles more vigorously as you inhale. Breathe consciously while the witness is answering. Take longer pauses between sentences to breathe deeper.

Helpful hint: Breathing from the belly will save your voice.

It is important to differentiate between two different kinds of deep breathing. The first is the slow, relaxing breath described in Chapter One. This is the conscious breathing you do prior to standing up to speak in court. As you sit at counsel table, warm up the muscles of respiration slowly, gently, and carefully. Use deliberate, deep breathing to calm your emotions as well as to prepare to channel the imminent adrenaline buzz. You have time to breathe when a witness is providing an extended answer during direct examination, when you pause to look at your notes, walk with purpose in silence to a new location, or simply stop to think. But when you're actually speaking, there isn't time for these slow, measured inhalations; they simply take too long. Although this more vigorous breathing requires you to expend more energy while speaking in court, it also aids your body and brain's constant replenishment with oxygen to support and project your voice.

Breathe In and Speak Out

Take a breath, and on exhalation, speak. Don't misunderstand—this doesn't mean that you should inhale, exhale, and then try to speak. That cannot work, since your lungs would be empty when you needed to speak. Breathe in to fill your lungs, and once they're filled, use the air in your lungs to power your voice.

From the dawn of time until the advent of the microphone, public speakers had to be able to project their voices at great volume. Imagine Caesar addressing the Roman legions, or Lincoln delivering the *Gettysburg Address* to twenty thousand listeners—outdoors and without amplification! It is almost inconceivable that they managed to be heard beyond the first rows. Yet they *were* heard. They had breath control techniques that enabled them to project their voices loudly and for long periods of time.

Today there remain some stage performers with extraordinary breath control and volume, but theirs is a dying art. Classical singers and stage actors are still trained to be loud enough to project to the last row of the balcony. Opera singers, in particular, are the Olympians of musicmaking—the sheer strength of the compressed air in their lungs allows them to be heard over an entire symphony orchestra. The stereotype of fat opera singers does have a kernel of truth, in fact. That extra weight becomes ballast for the remarkable breath support necessary to produce loud, ringing high notes. When they take in a deep, abdominal breath, their extra body weight helps the abdominal wall drop forward, flattening the diaphragm and pulling a large volume of air into the lungs. This air is then compressed by the power of the working abdominals, diaphragm, and intercostals, which push it back up and through the larynx, where the vocal cords vibrate. The length of vocal cords determines voice type and range. Whether a resonant *basso profundo* or a high tenor, a mellow alto or a dynamic soprano, all big voices are powered by muscle and practice.

This type of muscular breathing has direct applications in the courtroom. You may need to fill a large space with your unamplified voice, and be heard by the judge, witness, and the hard-of-hearing elderly members of the jury. Only consistent breath control makes every word audible. On cross-examination, for example, the important word is usually at the end of the question: "Captain McCarthy, you did not call for help for three hours." It is natural (here's the paradox again) for your voice to trail off at the end as you run short of breath and your voice drops to a lower pitch. But you can't leave the jury wondering how long it took Captain McCarthy to call for help. This is important, or you wouldn't be asking the question. To be loud enough, do what singers and actors do. Use your abdominal and rib cage muscles to stay loud—or get louder—as the question comes to an end.

Your Larynx and Vocal Cords

Your diaphragm pushes air up and out your lungs so that it flows up your trachea, or windpipe, to your larynx. The larynx is the "voice box" in which your vocal cords are housed. Though sometimes pictured as two thick rubber bands stretched across your larynx, the vocal cords really aren't cords. They are two folds of cartilage attached to the sides of your larynx with a space between them. When you speak, air passes through the folds, causing them to vibrate. The greater the amount of air passing across your vocal cords, the greater the volume (or, in technical terms, the decibel level) of your voice. A very soft whisper uses so little air that the cords don't vibrate, while a full-throated shout causes them to vibrate vigorously.

Manipulating your larynx will not increase the volume of your voice. If you add unnecessary tension to your neck, throat, and vocal cords, you will only limit your volume (and possibly damage your vocal cords). Keep your neck and throat relaxed so that air can pass across your vocal cords unimpeded by excess tension. The more open, relaxed, and properly aligned your neck and larynx, the more freely, easily, and vigorously your vocal cords can vibrate.

It's difficult to gain technical control over the vocal cords, since you can't look directly at them. You must rely on physical sensation. Some voice teachers compare the feeling of an open throat to the sensation felt when inhaling quickly and deeply in a gasp of amazement. With your fingers placed gently on your larynx, take in a vigorous inhalation of surprise. Feel how the larynx moves downward as the throat opens. That is the feeling you seek – a relaxed, open throat.

Articulators and Articulation

The articulators—your jaw, lips, and tongue (which interacts with your teeth)—transform a column of vibrating air into intelligible words. Furthermore, your face has 44 different muscles, a large number of which are involved in enunciation and articulation. The more energetically and precisely you work these muscles, the more easily the jury can understand you.

In conversational speech, articulators are often underused, and many syllables and consonants—especially final consonants—are dropped in conversation. Although we write:

Q: When are you going?
A: I'm going to leave about nine.

We often say this, using fewer syllables and dropped consonants:

> When ya goin'?
> I'm gon' leave 'bout nine.

In conversation, the context and melodic contour of a sentence helps people understand each other. Lack of articulation generally isn't a problem. To be understood in the courtroom, however, you must give each consonant its proper enunciation. Taste every consonant. Savor them, even those you may drop in conversation.

Regional Accents

In many regional accents in spoken American English, consonants are dropped and vowels formed in distinctive ways. Only an authentic "Noo Yawker" would give you directions to the intersection of "Toidy toid street 'n' Toid Avenoo." Bostonians have a unique way with the letter "r," which they sometimes drop altogether—"Let's meet in Hava'd Ya'd"—and sometimes add where it isn't written, as in "Havana, Cubar." Southern accents often stretch vowels, adding additional syllables that are not to be found on the printed page. A distinguishing characteristic of the Upper Midwest accent is the tendency to turn the "ing" sound into "een," with a cheerful "Good morneen!" They also unconsciously tend to contract contractions. The words "did not" can be shortened to "didn't," which is further contracted to make a one-syllable word: "di'n't." Thus, this regional accent leads to courtroom statements like, "My client di'n't do it; he cou'n't do it, and he wou'n't do it." But a Midwestern jury wo'un't think that sounded at all peculiar, because they talk with the same accent themselves.

If you relocate to a different region of the country or have to try a case in front of a jury far from your home accent, modifying your regionalisms may be an advantage. You can attenuate or eliminate some of the more pronounced markers of your regional accent, if you concentrate. But to do so, you need to be more conscious of your articulators and your articulation.

Remember: Taste every consonant and pronounce every syllable.

Warm Up to Be Articulate

The best way to achieve the clearest speech is to enunciate vigorously, paying attention to the small details of pronunciation. Elocution once was taught in grade schools, but now seems quaint. The word evokes visions of an overly formal style, taught by an uptight pedagogue with a starched lace collar and ramrod straight posture. Actors, singers and broadcasters still study diction, but for the rest of us, the study of declamation and delivery has pretty much gone out of style.

Nevertheless, speaking clearly in order to be understood in a courtroom requires precision. Think of your articulators as an important component of your technique. Warm them up before you speak, just as an athlete warms up prior to a competition. Prepare them to go to work immediately, and you are much less likely to trip over your own tongue at the start of your presentation. (Fluency errors early in a presentation have two downsides: they undermine your confidence and can make a negative first impression on the jury.)

Here are a number of ways to warm up. Find a private place and a couple of minutes to stretch and invigorate your articulators and the small muscles in your face. If you are now in a private place, stretch the muscles of your face to learn this technique.

Open your mouth as wide as possible; simultaneously, open your eyes and lift your eyebrows. (Don't be shy, no one is watching.) Stick out your tongue as well. Continue this stretching action by compressing the same muscles. Withdraw your tongue, and scrunch up your face by pursing your lips and squeezing your eyes closed. Now alternate between these two different actions. Stretch and then squeeze, stretch and then squeeze your facial muscles several times. Next, try to move all your facial muscles to the right side of your face, then to the left side. Lift all the facial muscles up, then down. Move your face around at random, stretching every muscle. Now stop, and feel the warm, subtle sensation of increased blood flow in those muscles. Warm up to be articulate right from the start.

Next, warm up the lips and the tip of the tongue. Repeat these nonsense syllables over and over, increasing the speed as you get more comfortable and warmed up:

niminy piminy, niminy piminy, niminy piminy (etc.)

To form the consonant "n," place the tip of your tongue behind your upper front teeth; the "m" and the "p" are formed by the lips. Take a deep breath and exaggerate as you articulate this pattern again. Work the articulators crisply and vigorously, more than you ultimately will use them while speaking. This will prepare you to speak clearly and easily. Say the same pattern again, this time moving the pitch of your voice from the lower register to the upper register. Move the pitch up and down to warm up your vocal cords as you warm up your articulators.

The next exercise works the articulators from front to back. Say:

butta gutta, butta gutta, butta gutta (etc.)

Say aloud the consonant "b" and feel how it is formed on the lips. "T " is formed with the tongue and teeth. The "guh" sound is formed in the back of your mouth when the back of your tongue arches up to meet the roof of your mouth. Repeat the exercise and feel the shifting of the consonants from your lips to the back of your mouth. Exaggerate and say it again, moving the pitch of your voice from lower to higher to lower to higher.

You also can warm up your articulators by using tongue twisters:

Peter Piper picked a peck of pickled peppers.

She sells seashells by the seashore.

Yet another way to warm up the articulators is to begin a mental list of words that trip your tongue. Collect those words and use them as a warm-up exercise. When you trip over words with consonants that you find personally challenging—perhaps the alternating "s" and "th" sounds of the word "anesthesiologist"—then use that word as a warm-up:

anesthesiologist, anesthesiologist, anesthesiologist (etc.)

Say it a number of times, exaggerating the articulation and gradu-ally increasing your speed.

Over articulate these warm-up exercises to increase the blood flow into the muscles of your face and to prepare to speak. Of course, you will not exaggerate your articulation as you speak in court, but it is the best way to warm up.

With the muscles of respiration and articulation warmed up and ready to work, the next step is to make choices about how you are go-ing to channel the energy these muscles provide. To make these choic-es, you first need to give yourself time, which leads us to a discussion of controlling the pace at which you speak.

Making Persuasive Choices

Speaking persuasively in court requires that you make verbal choices spontaneously. As you select the words to say, you must simultaneously decide which words to emphasize in order to make your meaning clear. In an opening statement, which sentence deserves extra emphasis? In a series of questions, which ones merit particular stress? Within each question, which words are most important? Much as you use a yellow highlighter on the printed page, you can use your voice to audibly highlight important words, clauses, and sentences. But it takes time to make these choices. Recall from Chapter Two that adrenaline slows time for you. Use that time—and the silent moments it provides— not only to think about what you are saying, but also how to say it expressively.

Silence is the secret ingredient of persuasive speech. If you are uncomfortable with silence, you will talk too fast; you won't take time to think about what you are saying, and your sentences will be awkwardly constructed and delivered. You will trip over your tongue. You speak first and think second, so your lips move and words are generated before your brain has decided what to say. Also, talking too fast often leads to an excessive use of thinking noises—*uh* and *um* and *OK*—as the brain struggles to find more time to think. Eventually your self-confidence collapses, and your train of thought threatens to crash and burn. Speaking persuasively, on the other hand, begins with controlling the pace at which you talk—and to do so, you must be comfortable with silence. (Recall from Chapter Two that if jurors don't have time to think about what you are saying, they won't remember it, much less be persuaded by it.)

Energy Up, Pace Down

Persuasive speech requires more energy than casual conversation. That is why being "natural" is not enough to get the job done, and why merely being comfortable as an advocate is not synonymous with being convincing. One source of the necessary energy for persuasive speech is your own adrenaline. It provides the body with extra energy to cope with potentially life-threatening situations. When people are anxious, they often refer to "coping with lots of nervous energy." Co-opt that feeling, and focus on the energy already available within you. Say to yourself, "Good! I'm nervous. That will provide me with extra energy—and energy is the raw material of communicating persuasively."

When you think of a speaker with lots of energy, you may suppose that energy and speed are synonymous: an energetic talker is a fast talker. Not necessarily. Energy can be used to speak quickly, but it can also be used to speak emphatically. When advocates speak persuasively, they use lots of energy—for emphasis and clarity, not speed. When people speak persuasively, they often become more energetic while simultaneously slowing their pace. The increase in energy signals the importance of what is being said, and the slower pace gives the listener time to think about, and be persuaded by, what is being said. The energy goes up and the pace goes down.

By warming up and using your breath and articulators, you raise your energy. To slow the pace, employ the concept of chunking. The brain functions best when it has time to formulate language in chunks; likewise, your jury understands better when it receives your message in small bits.

Speak in Phrases, Not Whole Sentences

In everyday conversation, you gather your thoughts into sentences constructed one chunk at a time. Words are grouped into phrases; phrases are arranged into bigger chunks, or sentences. On the written page, punctuation—commas, periods, question marks, exclamation points, dashes—signals a chunk's conclusion. Sentences composed around one idea are grouped into paragraphs, and larger paragraph chunks are delineated visually by indentation and added spacing.

At the very beginning of a presentation, when you most likely are feeling the time warp created by adrenaline, you should consciously speak in phrases and use small gaps of silence between them to think. The silence between phrases and sentences becomes an audible punctuation, signaling to listeners when the chunks begin and end. If there is no silence, there is no audible punctuation. Confusion ensues. Imagine the visual (and cognitive) challenge to a reader if this paragraph were printed as follows, without any punctuation:

at the very beginning of the presentation when you are most likely feeling the time warp created by adrenaline you should consciously speak in phrases and use small gaps of silence to think between them the silence between phrases and sentences becomes the audible punctuation that gives listeners ears signals about when the chunks begin and end if there is no silence there is no audible punctuation imagine this visual challenge to the reader if the following paragraph were printed with no punctuation at all

All the words are correct, but without proper punctuation it is much harder for the reader to parse and comprehend. Spoken language presents a similar challenge. Listeners need signals—audible punctuation—to mark when chunks start and stop. Whether these chunks are phrases, sentences, or paragraphs, their meaning becomes unambiguously clear through intermittent moments of silence.

Because of the adrenalized time warp, you don't have an accurate sense of what a slow or fast pace really is. Rely on speaking in phrases to give your brain sufficient time to construct each sentence or question carefully, one chunk at a time. Since the brain likes to think in chunks, this strategy fits perfectly with the jury's cognitive processing. This is not the same as speaking slowly in such a way that your creeping pace annoys the listener. Speaking slowly might suggest that you should move your articulators slowly, but that would sound ridiculous. (You... do... not... think... or... speak... one... word... at... a... time.) *Speak in phrases (not whole sentences)* is a more practical instruction for the brain to follow.

If you are a really fast talker with a rapid-fire, machine-gun delivery, control the pace by regularly taking your finger off the metaphorical trigger. Speak in phrases, and in the silence between them allow the fact finders to digest and be persuaded by what you have said. Although the words may fly out of your mouth, you still can give the listener time to process those verbal bursts.

Practice saying important sentences and questions at a slower pace to provide contrast. If you say everything at the same quick pace, then all sounds the same and appears to be of equal importance—and that is never true. To mark their significance, important utterances need to be spoken at a slower, more deliberate pace.

The Mechanics of Phrasing

Imagine the encounter when a parent, unhappy that a teenager has stayed out too late, attempts to persuade the errant teen not to do that again. The pace slows down; the energy level goes up. Speaking a phrase at a time and maintaining the energy level, the parent says emphatically:

> If you *ever*
> come home *again*
> *that* late,
> you
> will be *grounded*
> for a *month*.
> Are you *listening*?

Say that out loud, persuasively! Say it deliberately, one phrase at a time, and say it like you mean it. Say it like you heard it said to you, or like you yourself have said it.

Use your pace to signal the significance of the message; find a deliberate, speak-in-phrases rhythm that affords abundant time for it to sink in. Do not speak quickly. If this warning were delivered at a fast pace it would not sound as credible, nor be as convincing. In persuasive speech, energy is used to emphasize key words; the pace remains slow and deliberate.

We speak in phrases whenever we recite text together as a group. For instance, citizens of the United States are speaking in phrases when they recite the *Pledge of Allegiance*:

> I pledge allegiance
> to the flag
> of the United States of America,

and to the Republic
for which it stands,
one phrase
at a time...

The *Pledge* is a perfect, and familiar, example of speaking in phrases. Use it to set the proper pace at the beginning of every presentation. First, decide what you want to say, and then practice saying it with a deliberate pace modeled on the *Pledge of Allegiance*'s rhythm.

There are many well-known examples of orators speaking in phrases. In his Inaugural Address President John F. Kennedy challenged the nation with these words, delivered persuasively, one phrase at a time:

Ask not
what your country
can do for you;
ask what you
can do for your country.

If you recite that quotation aloud but say it quickly, it loses its power. When you say it slowly, and emphasize the key words, you begin to sense the power of speaking a phrase at a time. Say Kennedy's words aloud again, more slowly than before. Hear the short gaps of silence between the phrases. Stretch them even longer. The slower you speak, the more important the idea appears to be.

Vary the Pace

In court, you will not say everything a phrase at a time, slowly and deliberately. Speak in phrases when what you are saying is relatively important— when you want the jury to think carefully about what you are saying. As we discussed in Chapter Two, beginnings and endings of courtroom presentations should be carefully crafted (the significance of primacy and recency). Between these beginnings and endings, you'll want to speak in phrases whenever you say something particularly noteworthy, whether emphasizing facts in an opening or arguments in a closing, or asking key questions during examinations. You can talk faster when covering preliminary information. A transitional sentence such as, "Moving on to what happened on July 15...", would be a logical place to speak more quickly. The jury doesn't need to hear that transitional sentence a phrase at a time nor the preliminary information that follows. You will make choices constantly about how and when to vary your pace to fit your persuasive purpose.

Be flexible enough in your pacing to slow down and speak in phrases whenever you come to more crucial points. When you arrive at this information, state it a phrase at a time, slow the pace, and keep the energy high. This gives your jurors time to think about, remember, and be persuaded by what you are saying.

The necessary variation in pace—slow to fast to slow to fast—is analogous to the movement of a train pulling out of the station. Start speaking slowly to get your train of thought on track. That deliberate pace will signal significance to your jury, when they are paying close attention at the beginning. Inevitably you will speed up as you get going, like a train building a head of steam. Slow down again at each station—each important point along the way—to make certain your listeners are on board.

Since your brain composes sentences a phrase at a time, you are, in a sense, always speaking in phrases. When something is important, the gaps between those phrases become slightly elongated; there is more time, and hence more silence, between them. When you speak more briskly about preliminary or transitional matters, you still speak in phrases, but the gaps between the phrases grow shorter or disappear altogether.

Use Your First Utterances to Set the Pace

Each time you stand to speak in court, the first words out of your mouth will set the pace for what follows. Be careful, therefore, about rushing through your first few sentences:

May it please the court. This is a case of mistaken identity. Joshua Franklin was in another state on the night of the robbery.

Whether stating your theme or using common boilerplate, lawyers usually begin speaking very quickly. Boilerplate is rote information, and not as interesting as what follows. When your first utterance is too fast, that hasty tempo tends to persist, and it will prove hard to slow down when the more substantive sentences are reached.

To avoid this problem, practice the first sentences aloud. Consciously set a slower, more deliberate opening pace. Say it a phrase at a time, rather than tossing it off quickly. Say it as if it has real meaning, as if you are truly asking if it pleases the court for you to begin, rather than merely reciting a meaningless ritual. Stating your "grabber" theme, with proper emphasis and pace, exploits the moment of primacy, and gives you something truly important to say immediately.

Begin Sentences Deliberately

Once you are past boilerplate and have launched into substance, continue to control the pace. The advantage of speaking more deliberately, one phrase at a time, is that the slower pace, and the additional thinking time between phrases that it affords, gives you greater cognitive control. You literally have more time to consider what you are saying as you say it. If you lose your train of thought and need to stop and think, which still can happen even when speaking more slowly, the longer gaps between phrases or sentences that result will be much less evident. If you begin by adopting a delivery punctuated with short, frequent gaps between phrases and sentences, then when one of those gaps is slightly prolonged, it's hardly noticeable. The silences become a kind of insurance against the derailing of your train of thought, enabling you to recover and move ahead. We all begin sentences without knowing how they will end. Use silence to think your way through long, complex sentences without ever correcting a word.

Eliminate Thinking Noises

In conversational speech, many people constantly use the thinking noises *uh, um,* or *ah.* This is not an issue of intelligence or education; it's habit. Even highly educated speakers tend to use thinking noises far more often than they are aware. And awareness, or a lack thereof, is precisely the problem. Some speakers habitually use 10, 15, or even 20 *ums* per minute! (Try counting the *ums* a mediocre speaker uses; you'll be surprised by what you hear.) If you knew how often you do it, you'd be motivated to stop, or at least to reduce their frequency. But like all habits, this one is subconscious and reflexive, so you have no pressing reason to stop—except when you hear yourself on voice mail or an answering machine! It's no wonder that a problem so ingrained through daily repetition is difficult to control and eliminate.

Thinking noises are an excellent example of why you simply can't tell yourself to be natural, when being natural may very well include the excessive, annoying *ums, uhs, likes* and *you knows* of ordinary conversation. Once you're on your feet addressing a jury, it's too late to begin thinking about eliminating this persistent habit. You must work at changing it far in advance. Make it your goal to use no thinking noises at all—not in court, not in conference rooms, not on the phone, and not while talking to clients. Strive always to be the articulate attorney.

Thinking noises typically occur when you speak in phrases but don't use silences as punctuation. In the place of silence, you insert a one-second, monosyllabic *um.* This noise indicates that you know it's your turn to speak but you need a second to think of what to say next. Lasting almost always about one second, and occurring on the same musical pitch in the speaker's voice, thinking noises lend a monotone quality to speech that is both distracting and annoying.

Certain words also can function as thinking noises. The expression "you know," often inserted between phrases and sentences, gives the speaker an additional second to think. Children, teens, and even many adults use the word "like" in the same way. Nothing is *like* a clearer indication that *like* a person hasn't fully acknowledged *like* their professional status than this *like* annoying and childish verbal habit. Summer associates at law firms often are shocked to discover that speaking with this accent of adolescence is *like* highly undesirable. If you talk like a child, people don't take you seriously as a professional.

Another reason that thinking noises are *um* irritating is they intrude on the listener's thinking time. Just when your audience needs a second to consider what you have said, the thinking noise fills the silence like static on a cell phone connection. It interferes with the listener's cognitive processing. *Um* and *uh* are both irritating and counterproductive. Fortunately, they are also completely curable.

Remember, any thinking noise you are trying to eliminate is merely an audible indication that your brain needs a second to consider what you are about to say. You are verbalizing your need to stop—for one second—and think before speaking. The solution is to give your brain what it wants—a moment to think—but not to fill the needed silence with a bothersome and meaningless noise. Chapter Four, *How to Practice*, discusses in detail how to stop saying *um*.

Mind the Gap

Passengers in the London Underground system hear an announcement over the public address system whenever a train pulls into the station: "Mind the gap. Mind the gap." A pleasant woman's voice reminds passengers that there is a gap between the platform and the subway car. Use this phrase to help break the habit of thinking noises.

Make the phrase a reminder to yourself to insert a gap of silence between phrases. Then follow the instruction: mind the gap and pay attention! Do you have the urge to insert a thinking noise? Listen to the gap between phrases and sentences. This gap is a short pause, not necessarily a long rumination. During that brief moment, focus your mind on silence.

It is much easier to break a habit when you can give your brain a positive instruction, such as mind the gap, rather than a negative one: Don't say *um!* The negative instruction doesn't work because it keeps you focused on the problem, not the solution. Rather than telling yourself not to do something, tell yourself to do something better: *mind the gap.*

Helpful hint: To break verbal habits, focus on the solution by minding the gap.

Emphasis and Meaning

Speaking in phrases with plenty of silences helps you project your voice, speak clearly and precisely, compose coherent thoughts, and eliminate thinking noises. Adopting this deliberate pace is also an essential element of persuasion. Expressive, powerful speech takes time. If you talk too fast, there isn't much time to emphasize key words, which unlock the meaning of speech. Take the time to weigh word choice and expression. The accent you place on operative words can then be shaped to the maximum persuasive advantage.

Emphasis is vital for understanding speech. It is the *em*-pha-sis on the right *syl*-la-ble that makes words comprehensible. If someone speaks English with a heavy accent and places the em-*pha*-sis on the wrong syl-*lab*-le, it makes the listener's job more difficult. Intelligibility follows a progression: emphasis on the right syllable makes a word clear, and highlighting operative words makes a sentence understandable. Likewise, the proper emphasis on an important sentence makes a paragraph of thought cohesive, and stressing your most prominent points makes your entire argument persuasive. During examinations, giving special attention to key questions clarifies your line of questioning. Emphasis gives spoken language a clear and persuasive meaning.

Imagine that in a commercial dispute you spoke the following sentence to the jury: "She never promised the shipment would arrive by Tuesday." The meaning of that sentence will shift in subtle yet significant ways depending on which word you emphasize. Repeat this sentence aloud, emphasizing the key words printed in italics:

She never promised the shipment would arrive by Tuesday.
(maybe *he* did, but *she* didn't)

She *never* promised the shipment would arrive by Tuesday.
(with the stress on *never* it is an absolute denial)

She never *promised* the shipment would arrive by Tuesday.
(you are waffling with the emphasis on this word)

She never promised the *shipment* would arrive by Tuesday.
(maybe she promised the invoice, but not the *shipment*)

She never promised the shipment *would* arrive by Tuesday.
(it could have arrived, but delivery wasn't guaranteed)

She never promised the shipment would *arrive* by Tuesday.
(shipped on Tuesday, yes, but not arrive)

She never promised the shipment would arrive by *Tuesday*.
(maybe Wednesday, but not Tuesday)

And finally, one can also emphasize a number of different words in a single sentence:

She *never* promised the *shipment* would *arrive* by *Tuesday*.

This is what persuasive speech often sounds like.

An even subtler example of emphasis affecting meaning can be found in a famous quotation from Lincoln's *Gettysburg Address*:

...government of the people, by the people, and for the people...

That line usually is delivered with the emphasis on the prepositions *of*, *by*, and *for*:

> …government *of* the people, *by* the people, and *for* the people…

What happens to the meaning if you shift the emphasis to other words? Filmmaker Ken Burns did just that when directing actor Sam Waterston delivering the *Gettysburg Address* in his documentary, *The Civil War*. Burns believes that the proper emphasis is not on the prepositions but on the people:

> …government of the *people*, by the *people*, and for the *people*…

This shift in emphasis changes the meaning. The conspicuous repetition of the word "people" puts the emphasis, both literal and philosophical, in a different place. Say it aloud to get the feel of it.

The art of acting rests largely on the power of emphasis to clarify and enrich meaning. The playwright writes the words, and the actor speaks those lines as written. But the actor (together with the director) decides which words to emphasize. In *Death of a Salesman*, playwright Arthur Miller has Linda, wife of the salesman Willie Loman, say of her husband's desperate plight, "Attention must be paid." The playwright doesn't indicate which of those words should be emphasized; the actor must decide.

> *Attention* must be paid.
> Attention *must* be paid.
> Attention must be *paid*.

Or perhaps every word in that short sentence is worthy of emphasis:

> *Attention…must…be…paid.*

Because acting is an art and not a science, all these choices are possible. Using their trained voices, actors make such choices by the thousands, and these ultimately coalesce into an interpretation of a role.

Advocacy, too, is an art—one in which you must decide which words to highlight in order to convey your intended meaning. But the enormous difference between acting and advocating is that you do not recite from memory as actors do; you think on your feet. You make extemporaneous choices about emphasis. You do this all the time in conversation without a thought. Virtually every sentence you utter has at least one and often several words that you emphasize instinctively. Start listening to yourself and to others; hear accent, nuance, and expression in conversation.

Volume, Pitch and Duration

Emphasis can be applied to words by varying volume, pitch, and duration. Often we stress the key words in a sentence by simply saying them louder. Say aloud this phrase from the *Gettysburg Address*, speaking the italicized words louder:

> …government of the *people*, by the *people*, and for the *people*…

Now say it aloud the traditional way, stressing the prepositions:

> …government *of* the people, *by* the people, and *for* the people…

Try doing just the opposite with the volume of your voice. Stress the key words by saying them more softly (but still intensely) compared to the other words.

> …government *of* the people, *by* the people, and *for* the people…

Emphasis also can be accomplished with pitch. Repeat our example using a higher pitch on the key words. This is the way we usually hear this famous quotation spoken. Now invert the intonation, using a lower pitch on the key words:

> …government *of* the people, *by* the people, and *for* the people…

Repeat these words yet again, using first a higher pitch and then a lower pitch to emphasize the italicized words:

…a government of the *people*, by the *people*, and for the *people*…

If you have trouble hearing your own voice navigate the subtleties of pitch variation, make an audio or video of yourself. (You may be able to use a cell phone for this.)

Emphasis also can be achieved with duration—by elongating the vowel of the accented syllable in the key word. Written language sometimes imitates this practice. Think of the different meanings of these words on a printed page:

Terse: No.

Emphatic: Nooo.

Hysterical: Nooooooo!

The repeated letter represents a prolongation of the vowel sound. Even in conversational speech, we often emphasize a word by slightly elongating accented vowel sounds. Listen to a recording of "I Have a Dream," Martin Luther King Jr.'s celebrated speech on civil rights. In it, he frequently emphasizes words by stretching their vowels:

I have a *dream*, that one day this nation will *rise* up and *live* out the *true* meaning of its *creed*: "We hold these *truths* to be *self-*evident: that *all* men are created *equal*."

Say this quotation aloud, slowly and deliberately. Speak it in phrases so that you have the time necessary to elongate the vowels of the words in italics. Then say it again, even slower, and stretch the vowels a bit more. Do you notice how the *pace* at which you speak is related to the *time* you have to be expressive with the words?

Likewise, President John F. Kennedy drew out the vowels of key words in his Inaugural Address:

Ask *not* what your *country* can do for *you*; ask what *you* can do for your *country*.

Say this quotation aloud, speaking it in phrases and emphasizing the key words—especially "you"—by prolonging their vowels.

You can, of course, read these excerpts in two very different ways. You can read the words simply, with no attempt to capture their inspirational meaning. In such a rendition, every word is given roughly equal weight. Alternatively, you can focus on their meaning by emphasizing key words. Such an emphatic, expressive delivery will allow you to convey the meaning behind the words, and not merely the words themselves. Don't just speak the text; you must speak the *meaning* of those words. Proclaim it, with commitment.

Unlike the orators cited above, you won't write out your courtroom presentations in advance and then read them to the jury. You will think on your feet, make choices about the words to use, and decide which ones need extra emphasis and intensity. Persuade your jury by varying the volume, pitch, and duration. You will be living, thinking, and speaking in the present moment—and that's fun!

Henry the Monotonous

Henry, an attorney for a Texas utility company, cross-examined a fire chief at a trial skills program. Henry asked his questions with a furrowed brow and little other expression, his voice fading and trailing off at the ends:

> Mr. O'Neil, you testified that you found Mr. Vashek's background disquieting.

Each question Henry asked sounded just like the one before. His voice was not perfectly monotone, but it was certainly monotonous, with an unvarying, repetitious drone. He spoke each question at the same pace. The amplitude of his voice stayed within a narrow range. His questions were good, but listening to them was tedious and boring.

At the lunch break, Henry struck up a conversation with Marsha Hunter. Her morning lecture had included a story about the adrenaline rush during an engine failure in a small plane. Henry had lots of questions about it: "Do you still fly?" "I was a flight instructor, but I never experienced a real emergency! That must have been scary!" He was animated, listened intently, and asked follow-up questions with keen interest.

Coincidentally, Henry had a private video review right after lunch. Watching his video, Henry was dismayed at how dull he was. Marsha asked him to remember how excited he'd been about her airplane story, and to infuse his examination with the enthusiasm that took his voice from its highs to its lows. The juxtaposition of Henry's lunchtime conversation with his dispiriting video did the trick for him. He got up and did the cross-examination again, and this time found variety, expression, and persuasion in his voice.

Remember: It isn't what you say. It's how you say it, and how emphatic you are.

Why Not Just Read?

As we discussed in Chapter Two, humans are not very good at reading aloud. Unless you are experienced at reading aloud and have a well developed, reliable technique for doing it convincingly, you won't be able to pull it off with any finesse. Why would you jeopardize your client's cause by relying on a specialized skill that you haven't cultivated?

Still, the urge to read in court is strong, and occasionally an experienced advocate will consider reading under certain circumstances. One seasoned litigator working on an emotionally wrenching case involving a truck accident worried the facts were so devastating that he might not be able to get through his opening unless he read it to the jury. Given these varied opinions, let's delve further into the question of reading.

We all read constantly. We spend our days reading, in fact. But reading silently is a very different skill from reading aloud persuasively. Indeed, all the hours that you've spent reading silently are a large part of the problem you face when attempting to read aloud. When you read silently, you tend to read very fast, and you'll probably read too fast when you read aloud. Most people do.

The faster you speak, the more likely you are to trip over your tongue and to read inexpressively. Key words won't receive the necessary emphasis; the music of your voice will sound stilted and flat, as though you're reading rather than talking—which you are! If reading aloud were easy, then virtually every literate person would be an effective actor or orator. Everyone would be able to pick up a script or speech and read it aloud with fluency and sincerity. But literacy and fluency are not equivalents. More to the point, even if you were a skilled reader, reading would be the wrong medium for persuasive advocacy.

When you read aloud, the music of your voice betrays that you are reading. Your range of expression narrows as you employ more limited vocal means. Your voice falls into repetitive patterns that quickly become boring.

There is another pitfall for an advocate who chooses to read. Your writing style is different from your speaking style. Even if you took the necessary time to practice reading slowly and carefully, it would be difficult to sound convincing because of this stylistic difference. You neither speak the way you write nor write the way you speak. So even if you could read aloud effectively, your writing style (especially after law school has trained you to write like a lawyer) will sound stilted and overly formal when spoken aloud.

Imagine this scenario: you have decided to write out, and read aloud, your closing argument. As the trial draws to a close, you plan to draft your closing argument that evening and deliver it the following morning. But the trial ends earlier than expected, and the judge says, "Counsel, rather than adjourn and present closing arguments tomorrow morning, let's finish up this afternoon. Please proceed with your closing arguments." You cannot respond, "Sorry, your honor, but I haven't written my closing argument yet. So I can't do it now." You must have the ability to think on your feet and deliver that closing by talking directly to the jury—not by reading to them.

But the best reason not to read in court is that it makes you less persuasive than when you are talking. Most likely you will stand at the lectern, stare at your notes, and periodically glance up furtively, in a way that no one in the jury mistakes for eye contact. You can't make sustained eye contact when you read. You've got to look the jurors in the eye, and you simply can't do that if you are reading to them. You may need to look at them, tell them the kindergartner watched as his father took his last breath before the paramedics could help, and then ask for damages. To do that, you need a technique for talking, not reading.

When You Must Read

Although reading is inconsistent with persuasion, there are times in court when you must read aloud: from a witness statement, for example, or from a deposition, expert's report, or written text projected onto a screen. When you're obliged to read aloud, read in phrases—slowly. Be aware that your brain, accustomed to reading silently and quickly, will be tempted to read too fast. Read deliberately, a phrase at a time, if you want jurors to fully comprehend the meaning of those words. Adopt a slow, deliberate pace and carefully emphasize key words to express yourself clearly.

You now have an understanding of how to breathe, project your voice, and articulate your words. In addition, you can coordinate your brain and voice by speaking in phrases, minding the gap between phrases and sentences, and emphasizing key words with volume, pitch, and duration to make your meaning clear.

Now, back to gesture! What do you do with your hands to highlight persuasive speech?

Gestures and Emphasis

Your body not only powers and projects your voice with breath from the lungs, it also directs the expressivity of your voice through gestures. The instinct to gesture expressively is connected with the emphatic stress of key words in a sentence or question. As the gesture research of Dr. Jana Iverson has revealed, "…gesturing and speaking are tightly connected in some very fundamental way in our brains."

Look for this connection in your own style. Using a video recording of a courtroom presentation you have made, look at your hands and listen to your voice. Place a sticky note on the television screen so that it hides your face from view, forcing you to focus on your gestures. Observe that your hands instinctively know which words deserve emphasis. Even when your fingers or wrist reveal only the slightest impulse to gesture, those impulses occur on key words. These impulses are not merely random fidgeting. Your hands know what to do. Trust them.

Gestures, as you'll recall from Chapter One, make you look and feel natural. But perhaps the foremost reason to liberate your instinct to gesture is to help your voice sound natural. Gesture makes your words and ideas clear and ultimately persuasive. Your hands know which words deserve emphasis and which vowels need to be stretched to achieve that. When you don't gesture, your vocal delivery suffers, and so do your listeners. While gesturing has a lot to do with how you look and feel as an advocate, it has an even larger role in how you sound. You could go so far as to say that listeners hear gestures—not the action of the gestures themselves, obviously, but the impact of those gestures on your speech pattern.

Monotone

The absence of gestures leads to an absence of emphasis on key words. Without emphasis on key words, the meaning of all words remains unclear—and you can't be persuasive if your meaning is not clear. Speech with no emphasis on key words slips easily into monotone—a difficult-to-listen-to, continuous stream of language stripped of the cues listeners need to grasp meaning. Monotone is literally mono-tonous, taking place all on one musical pitch.

Nobody—or more precisely *no body*—speaks in a monotone voice while gesturing. Monotone speech is always devoid of gestures. The next time you must endure a boring monotone speaker, transform your suffering into a learning experience. Ask yourself: Is she or he gesturing while speaking in that boring monotone? Take your eyes off the speaker's face and focus on the hands. You will see that monotone speech is linked to a lack of gesture. It follows that one good way to avoid speaking in a monotone is to speak with your hands and use your gestures.

Conduct Yourself

The speed of your gestures has a direct impact on the pace of your speech. When your hands move quickly, you talk fast. If your hands move slowly and smoothly, your pace slows too. As you speak, use your gesture to shape the language in much the same way that an orchestra conductor shapes Mozart or Stravinsky. The speed with which the conductor moves his arms dictates the tempo at which the music is played. The connection between the speed of gesturing and the speed of talking is powerful: it is virtually impossible to gesture quickly while talking slowly. So if you want to slow the pace at which you speak, gesture more slowly and smoothly. Conduct yourself to control the pace.

Be Smooth

Smoothness characterizes the gestures and pace of a natural, comfortable speaker. Her movements are not fast and jerky; they are slow and smooth, and her pace of speaking is slower and smoother as a result.

This connection between the speed of gesturing and the pace of speaking is especially important at the very beginning of a presentation. It is important to start gesturing immediately, using movements that are slow, smooth, and expansive. If you do not, your inhibited and restrained initial gestural impulse will lead to small, fast, jerky mini-gestures, which will lead you to speak too quickly. Your train of thought will be more likely to derail, and you will make a weaker first impression on the jury.

If you begin gesturing as soon as you speak, your natural gestures will make you look and feel comfortable, and will help you speak at a measured and deliberate pace. You will have more time to say carefully what you want to say. Hence you will look, sound, feel, think, and speak more effectively right from the start. The positive first impression you make will grab the jury's attention.

The secret of coordinating gestures and words at the proper pace is to practice this complex multi-tasking challenge alone, aloud, and on your feet. Don't leave beginnings to chance and inspiration.

Practice Beginnings with Gestures

Decide, in advance, exactly what you are going to say at the beginning of your presentation. This is one of the few times that you should practice saying verbatim—word-for-word—what you want to say in the first few sentences. Do not trust that on the spur of the moment you will spontaneously say exactly the right thing. It won't happen. (And you leave yourself vulnerable to saying something you regret. It is often at unplanned, spontaneous beginnings that speakers say awkward, inappropriate, or downright embarrassing things.)

Once you have found the precise wording of the very first sentences, then think about how to match your gestures to your words and ideas. This coordination, described in the discussion of jump-starting your gestures in Chapter One, involves deciding what words and ideas you will place "on the shelf" of gesturing. Remember that this invisible, imaginary shelf is where you place your hands in the ready position prior to speaking. Once you begin to speak, your gestures occur at and on this waist-high shelf. Plan logical gestures at the beginning.

You may decide that gesturing on the introductory boilerplate ("May it please the court, your honor, counsel, members of the jury...") doesn't feel quite right, although it is possible to gesture naturally even on the boilerplate. But immediately after that, what is the first substantive sentence you will say? In an opening statement it may be:

This is a case about *broken promises*, promises made in a *written contract*.

Thinking logically, you have two subjects, *broken promises* and a *written contract*. As you say this sentence, place *broken promises* on the one hand, and *written contract* on the other. Try that, and see how it feels to put those two concepts on the shelf. Logically connect your gestures to what you are saying, so they function as a visual aid for the jury. Emphasizing key words lets your jury see what you're talking about: a broken promise, on the one hand, and a written contract, on the other.

When you end your first substantive sentence with your body in this open and loose position, you send important symbolic messages to your jury in their first impression of you. The open position of the body says: "Trust me, I'm being open with you. I'm not hiding anything. I'm loose and natural, not uptight and stiff." In addition, you have jump-started your body's instinct to gesture, freeing your brain from any need to worry about what your hands are doing. Think about and practice your initial gestures so that you can quit thinking about them. Instinct will take over when you gesture immediately.

Here is another example. Direct examination may begin with this instruction to your witness:

Please introduce yourself to the members of the jury.

Gesture toward the witness with one hand, as you say *yourself*, and toward *the jury* with the other.

A cross examination might begin with this question to an arson expert:

> Mr. Tomkins, *you* never went to the *scene* of the fire, did you?

Gesture on the words *you* and *scene*. Alternatively, you could simply use an expansive, palms up questioning gesture that opens as you emphasize the word *you* and remains open until the question ends.

Finally, closing argument often begins with a strong restatement of your persuasive theme. In a dispute between an inventor and the corporation that licensed his invention, the inventor's counsel might begin his closing argument by saying:

> They *licensed* his inventions, made *millions* of dollars, and now
> they *refuse* to pay him the royalties he deserves.

This three-part theme could be placed on the shelf of gesture using three gestures in three different locations while emphasizing the words *licensed, millions,* and *refuse*.

Once you've decided what you intend to say to begin, and which gesture will fit logically with those words, practice to get the feel of coordinating words with gestures. Thinking about your choice is not sufficient. Your muscles need to feel the action. Stand up in a room alone and speak aloud.

Practice so your gestures and your voice have muscle memory. Thinking about gesturing isn't enough; you must practice. (More about muscle memory in Chapter Four.)

There is one more thing you can do while sitting at counsel table to prepare your muscles to gesture immediately and naturally. This mental preparation for physical activity is borrowed from sports psychologists.

Visualize Your Performance

Sports psychologists advise athletes to visualize their actions prior to competing. Athletes practice what they call "mental rehearsal." The Olympic skier imagines the moment when the buzzer sounds and she pushes off to plunge down the mountain in the giant slalom. The sprinter sees the moment when the starting gun goes off and he explodes out of the starting blocks. As an advocate, you can sit at counsel table and visualize the initial gestures you practiced. Visualizing an action that has been ingrained through practice frees you to gesture with even greater skill and confidence.

Athletes warm up and loosen up physically until right before a competition commences. Sitting in a courtroom, you don't have that same luxury. You may have to sit at counsel table for a long time before you get to stand up and speak. Even if you warmed up prior to walking into the courtroom, sitting for a long time will cool you down again. Visualization will help you to be ready when finally the judge says, "Counsel, you may proceed." As you sit there, think of the words you will say at the very beginning. See in your mind's eye the gestures you'll use to accompany those words. Hear the pace of speaking in phrases in your mind's ear, and see the slow, smooth gestures that will accompany those words in your mind's eye. Athletes use this visualization technique to win medals; you can use the same technique to win verdicts for your clients.

Prosody: The Music of Natural Conversation

Prosody is a general term for the musical elements of everyday speech. It encompasses tempo, rhythm, loudness, silence, and intonation. These musical elements interact with syntax and meaning as you speak. We have examined some musical features already: tempo or pace, and emphasis on key words lends a natural rhythmic cadence; loudness; and silence. This leaves intonation as the final element of prosody necessary for persuasive speech.

Intonation refers to the up-and-down movement of the musical pitch of your voice. This movement creates the subtle melody of natural speech. We have touched on the dreaded monotone, which lacks all melody or movement. Let's explore the desirable, persuasive alternative. No matter whether your voice is naturally pitched higher (soprano or tenor) or lower (alto or bass), you instinctively use a range of musical pitches as you speak, encompassing a lower, middle, and upper register. To speak persuasively you need the technical ability to make periodic choices about the intonation and pitch of your voice.

Fortunately, much of the necessary variation of intonation or pitch results from simply emphasizing key words in a phrase or sentence. The very act of emphasis leads your voice to vary the pitch appropriately. That being the case, now focus your attention on the intonation or pitch direction of your voice at the end of a sentence or question. Whether your voice is descending to a lower pitch or ascending to a higher one as the sentence or question ends, intonation affects the persuasive power and meaning of your words.

Walking Up and Down the Steps of Intonation

Compare the movement of your voice's pitch at the end of a sentence to going up or down the steps of a staircase. When your voice descends to a lower pitch, it seems to walk down the steps, and when it ascends to a higher pitch, it walks up the steps. Imagine that your voice has three levels, like a house with a main floor, basement, and attic. The middle pitches are the main floor where you spend most of your time. Your voice also has a basement and an attic where you go once in a while, but you don't spend as much time there as you do on the main floor.

Here is a familiar example: your voice naturally indicates finality by walking down the steps to a lower pitch. Say aloud the final phrase of the *Pledge of Allegiance* and listen to your natural intonation:

...with liberty and justice for all.

Because that is the end of the *Pledge,* your voice naturally indicates finality and closure by descending to a lower pitch. The descent provides audible punctuation, with the pitch of your voice placing a period at the end of the sentence:

...with liberty and justice for all [period].

To make this stepwise descent visual, we can notate the downward, stepwise progression like this:

...with liberty and
      justice for
         all.

Say this example aloud several times until you can confidently make your own voice walk down the steps. Once you can manipulate your voice in this way, use that same pattern, walking down the steps as you say:

Ab-so-
    lutely
      not!

Here is another familiar example of this descending pitch pattern. Broadcast journalists on radio and television walk down the steps at the end of every news report when they sign off by saying their name, news organization, and location. That descent looks and sounds like this:

Cokie Roberts,
    ABC News,
      Washington.

Imitate this familiar pattern. Sign off as a broadcaster, walking down the steps in this descending pattern. With that intonation pattern confidently in your voice and ear, use it to say:

> The defendant
>   refuses to take
>   responsibility.

Walk down the steps as you say:

> Use your
>   common
>   sense.

As you descend to a lower pitch, don't force your voice into an uncomfortable or unnatural range. These variations in pitch take place within your natural vocal range and should not sound forced or artificial. If they do, you are pushing your voice too low.

In a subtle yet significant way, walking down the steps at the end of a sentence conveys confidence and finality. If you expect to persuade your jury, you have to sound like you believe what you are saying and are confident in your case. This pattern helps to achieve that goal.

The other advantage to walking down the steps is that the finality suggested by the descending pitch buys you some extra time to think about what to say next. Both to your jurors' ears and to your own, that descending pattern signals a conclusion. The sentence is finished. Period. Your jury has a little extra time to think about what you just said. The sound of finality will help you mind the gap between sentences because this intonation pattern makes the brain less inclined to fill in the gap with a thinking noise.

Walking down the steps is especially useful at the beginning of a presentation when you are tempted to talk too quickly. Walking down the steps will help you mind the gap, speak in phrases, and emphasize key words. Here's a printed notation of this pattern:

Compose your sentence
a phrase at a time,
and on the final phrase
walk
      down
           the steps.

Say that aloud, and do what you are saying.

If you begin a courtroom presentation with a series of sentences that end with this descending pattern, you immediately convey a sense of confidence and control. This puts you at ease as you employ the melody of power and persuasion, and also buys you time to think. And when you have enough time to think, you can say what you want to say clearly and persuasively.

Ending with Confidence

The law of primacy and recency tells us that listeners pay close attention to beginnings and endings. If endings are as important as beginnings, then you need a technique to signal reliably that you are finished. Whether saying the last sentence of a speech or the last question of an examination, walk down the steps to indicate that you are concluding. To reinforce the sense of finality, walk down the steps and slow down: go slower as you go lower. This powerfully conveys the message that you have finished.

You might end your opening statement with this plea:

Members of the jury, at the end of this trial we will ask you for
a verdict in favor of
      Acme
          Industries.

Say that aloud and end the sentence by going slower as you go lower. Keep the volume up until the last word. Don't confuse lowering your pitch with lowering your volume. Walking down the steps is also the intonational pattern of the leading questions you will most often use on cross-examination.

Walking Up the Steps

Walking up the steps takes the voice to a higher pitch at the end of a sentence, and this conveys a different meaning. This is the melody of exclamation, when your voice rises to a higher pitch. We indicate that additional energy on the printed page by ending the sentence with an exclamation mark: "I am shocked!" Spoken, it looks like this:

                shocked!
        am
    I

Speak that example aloud (with the requisite energy) and make your voice walk up the steps. Try this example of the audible exclamation mark used in conversation when you jokingly exclaim to a friend:

                mind!
        out of your
    You are

Walking up the steps is a pattern you will use less often than walking down the steps. If you overuse it you may sound like the stereotypical used car salesman. In fact, this pattern is used excessively in television commercials. Think of the huckster in the late night infomercial braying:

            tee it!
        guaran-
    I

But walking up the steps is useful in court. Use it to energetically de-clare your theme at the beginning of opening statement:

choices!

case about

This is a

You could also walk up the steps in closing argument. Walk up the steps as you say aloud to an imaginary jury:

guilty!

is not

Mr. Nelson

The additional energy of walking up the steps builds momentum, and establishes at once that you are wholly committed to what you are saying. It can also be a useful technique in the middle of a lengthy opening statement or closing argument when you need to add some energy and spark to regain the jury's attention. Walking up the steps provides an intentional infusion of vocal energy to win back a listener's wandering attention.

Don't fear that you'll be constantly thinking about the upward or downward intonation of your voice at the end of every sentence you utter. You won't. Only periodically will you consciously use a rising or falling intonation for the specific, persuasive purposes of adding energy and enthusiasm (by walking up the steps) and adding finality and conclusiveness (by walking down the steps).

The Questioning Curl

How would you say this monosyllable:

"Huh?" ↝

This melody sliding upward, sometimes called an uptick, has different linguistic uses. Beware—use it carefully, because if it creeps into your language when you aren't paying attention, it can make you sound unsure of yourself. Listen to what happens to the sound of the vowel as you speak. When your voice slides upward on the vowel sound of a word, the sound suggests a question, right? Right? We call this intonation pattern the questioning curl because the musical pitch curls upward at the end. Say these phrases aloud and hear the difference between the questioning curl on the vowel of the final word, and walking down the steps in response:

Am I right? ↜

And the affirming answer:

You are right. ↷

Or more graphically…

    You
        are
            right. ↷

It is important to understand the difference between walking up the steps to the exclamation mark and the subtle upward slide of the questioning curl. The difference is the upward curl or slide of the pitch on the vowel. This curl does not happen when walking up the steps to the exclamation.

The questioning curl can turn a declarative sentence into a question. The declarative:

You went home.

with a questioning curl on the last word becomes:

                        e? ↜
                m
        o
You went h

Say these two examples aloud and hear the difference.

Use the questioning curl when asking open-ended questions that begin with the interrogative words *who, what, when, where, why, which,* or *how.* Ask the following questions aloud, and as you do, end each one with the questioning curl:

Who were you with? ↶
What did you do? ↶
When did you return? ↶
Where did you go? ↶
Why did you go there? ↶
Which route did you take? ↶
How did you get home? ↶

You also can ask these same questions by walking down the steps with your voice. Say the questions aloud, walking down the steps as you do so. Then repeat them, and walk up the steps. Walking up the steps, when asking an open-ended question, adds a sense of urgency to the delivery, as when a parent interrogates a child.

Who were you with?
What did you do?
When did you return?
Where did you go?
Why did you go there?
Which route did you take?
How did you get home?

Ask these questions one final time, but this time mix up your choices and use all three options: walk up the steps, walk down the steps, and use the questioning curl. Hear the subtle melodic differences. Don't be surprised if you find this challenging. Many people have never thought about the musical pitch patterns of speech, much less attempted to control and manipulate those patterns. It simply takes some practice to get the feel of it.

Curling and Listing

When you say a list of items aloud, your voice does the same kind of upward curl on the vowel sound of each item in the list.

> Go to the store and get some milk, ↗ eggs, ↗ bread, ↗ and coffee. ↘

Say that sentence aloud and hear how your voice slides upward on the vowel sounds of "…milk ↗, eggs ↗, bread ↗…" and then finally descends on the last word of the list: "coffee ↘." This is our natural way of making an audible list, with the curl at the end of each item in the list indicating to the listener that more is coming.

This listing intonation can affect your voice unconsciously in trial advocacy: the questioning curl can make you sound unsure of yourself. When you first begin to speak, your brain begins to tick off items on your mental list of things you need to say, including the opening boilerplate. First on the list is the request of the court: "May it please the court?" Next is the acknowledgment of your opponent, "counsel," and the jury, "members of the jury." Because the brain conceives these introductory formalities as a list, an upward inflection just like the questioning curl is used for every item on the list:

> Robert Cooper ↗ was in the wrong place ↗ at the wrong time ↗.

Once established, this list-making, upward intonation pattern is apt to be extended into the first substantive sentence and potentially through the entire opening paragraph.

> May it please the court ↗
> Counsel ↗
> Members of the jury ↗
> My name is Jane Doe ↗
> Counsel for the defendant ↗

Although there is no conscious intention on the advocate's part to ask a series of questions or convey a lack of confidence, the listing inflection gives that impression. The jury's first impression is that this trial lawyer isn't very sure of himself. In fact, he sounds like he is questioning virtually everything being said, including his own name and his client's! So beware of the trap lurking in the repetitive listing inflection. To avoid this problem, use the introductory boilerplate as an opportunity to consciously and confidently walk down the steps.

> Robert Cooper ⌒↘
> was in the wrong place ⌒↘
>   at the wrong time. ⌒↘

> May it
> please the
>   court, ⌒↘
> counsel,
> members
>   of the
>   jury ⌒↘.

> My name is
> Jane
>   Doe,
> counsel
> for the
>   defendant. ⌒↘

This short-circuits any listing tendencies, and gets you started confidently, in command of the courtroom.

Along with the expressions *like* and *you know*, the upward curl is another form of the accent of adolescence. The repetitive use of the rising inflection at the end of declarative sentences suggests lack of certainty, confidence, and maturity. If you wish to be taken seriously, expunge this vocal habit from your courtroom delivery as well as your professional conversational style. To avoid questioning yourself, beware the questioning curl.

Tone as a Tactical Choice

Chapter Two discussed the need to pick an attitude, and then make that attitude a tactical choice. When you don't pick one, you will default to the general attitude of "serious"—and serious, although appropriate to the courtroom, quickly becomes boring and bland.

We have been using the word "pitch" to describe the musical pitch of your voice, whether high or low. The word "tone" can be synonymous with pitch, as it is when we discuss avoiding a monotone delivery. However, here we use "tone" to mean that element of vocal delivery that reflects the attitude of the speaker, as when we say that someone used a curious or scornful tone of voice.

Together, attitude and tone constitute the underlying, driving energy of your vocal delivery. Once you choose an attitude, your tone of voice adjusts to fit it. They go hand in hand, and both should be used consciously. If, for example, you choose to conduct a "soft cross" on a sympathetic older witness, you may choose "respectful of elders" as your attitude. Your tone would be deferential, measured, not too loud, and never impatient. Should the witness become difficult, however, you might change your tone to be firmer, respectfully at odds, or somewhat louder. Your attitude could stay the same by using phrases like, "with all due respect, sir...."

Practicing Verbal Skills

Fortunately, you speak every day of your life, and this affords you abundant opportunities to practice regularly outside the pressurized environment of the courtroom. For example, you can practice eliminating thinking noises during a casual conversation with a friend. That is the perfect time to focus some of your attention on eliminating the *um* and *uh* as you mind the gap. Do you find yourself regularly stuck in traffic? What an opportunity to practice any of these elements of style (except gestures!). When you find yourself becalmed on the expressway, look at the clock on the dashboard and tell yourself to practice speaking without thinking noises for the next ten minutes. Then hold yourself to that obligation. Talk aloud for a full ten minutes and focus on eliminating thinking noises. When you hear yourself utter an *um* or *uh,* note that it happened, but don't stop and chastise yourself. Correct yourself and continue.

Don't be shy! With the advent of cell phones, many people constantly appear to be talking to themselves. If other drivers notice you talking to yourself, they won't know that you are practicing for a trial. They will assume you are talking on a hands-free cell phone.

Brief, regular practice sessions are more valuable than less-frequent, longer periods of practice time. Since so much of the challenge of speaking effectively is getting started, the more often you practice, the better you'll become at the hard part: the beginning.

You can even practice these speaking skills on the phone. Put a sticky note with the icon of the stair-step pattern on your phone, so that every time you reach for the phone that icon reminds you that you will sound more confident and in control if you walk down the steps at the ends of sentences.

Summary

To use your voice persuasively in the courtroom requires that you learn how to listen to yourself objectively. Get over the notion that you sound funny; you don't. You need to know how you use your voice expressively and persuasively outside the courtroom before you can replicate that naturalness inside the courtroom.

The power of your voice comes from the muscles of respiration, including the diaphragm and intercostal muscles, working with the abdominal muscles. Clarity of articulation is achieved with the vigorous precision of the articulators: the lips, teeth, jaw, and tongue interacting with the teeth. When you work the muscles of respiration and articulation harder, your juror's job is easier. Use audible punctuation to signal when phrases, sentences, and paragraphs have ended. Stressing the key words in your sentences and questions unlocks the meaning you intend. Emphasis is a function of volume, pitch, and duration.

The music of speech interacts with the meaning of your words. You can exploit this by walking down the steps to sound confident and conclusive, or walking up the steps to exclaim with greater energy. The questioning curl is a subtle use of intonation in which the pitch slides upward on the last word of a sentence or question. We use this pattern to ask questions and to make lists.

Diligently practice the skills outlined in this chapter to savor the power and pleasure inherent in the art of advocacy.

Mantras of Self-Instruction

☐ Taste every consonant.

☐ Give them a second.

☐ Raise the energy.

☐ Slow down the pace.

☐ Speak in phrases, not whole sentences.

☐ Use your first utterances to set the pace.

☐ Hear the silence, then use it.

☐ Silence is insurance.

☐ Mind the gap.

☐ Emphasize key words.

☐ Vary the volume, pitch, or duration.

☐ Conduct yourself slowly and smoothly.

☐ Put key words on the shelf.

☐ Gesture immediately.

☐ Visualize your performance.

☐ Walk down the steps.

☐ Go slower as you go lower.

☐ Walk up the steps.

☐ Beware the questioning curl.

☐ Tone of voice is a tactical choice.

☐ Obey the law of opposites.

☐ Practice alone, aloud, a lot.

CHAPTER FOUR

How to Practice

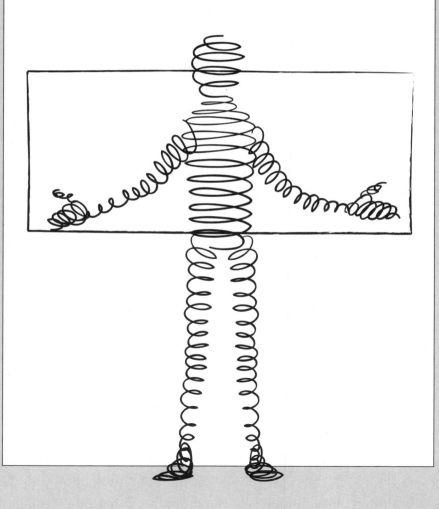

Practice is the path to expertise. It is the only way to improve skill in any discipline. The more complex the skill, the more practice is required. Whether you want to be a better golfer, pianist, or trial advocate, solitary, mindful practice is absolutely essential. "Practice makes perfect" is an endlessly repeated adage, and few would be foolish enough to argue the opposite: that you could acquire and improve a skill just by thinking, reading, or writing about it. Yet a surprising number of advocates don't practice—alone and aloud—the skills of advocacy. Practice, it turns out, is surprisingly hard work, difficult to fit into a busy lawyer's life. If you don't know how to practice efficiently and effectively, this hard work can be intimidating (and, like admonitions to exercise every day, easy to avoid). For some people, practice isn't so much intimidating as it is silly. Others find it downright embarrassing. Yet if you want to be a better trial lawyer, you must overcome any resistance you feel and learn how to practice.

Practicing is a skill in and of itself—arguably the ultimate skill. If you know how to practice, you can improve any skill you set your mind—and body—to learning. This chapter will guide you step-by-step through the required skills, and you'll learn to practice smarter, with better results in less time.

Some advocates want to believe that adequate preparation for trial advocacy can occur somehow without practice as the final, culminating step of that preparation. When asked how they prepared for a trial or trial advocacy training exercise, a surprising number of advocates confessed that they: 1) read carefully through the material (silently); 2) thought about it; 3) wrote copious notes on a legal pad; and 4) prayed that all their reading, thinking, and writing would somehow coalesce into articulate, persuasive speech, on the first attempt, under pressure in the courtroom. Don't put your trust in this self-delusion.

How can you prepare for speaking without *actually speaking*? Lawyers often rationalize: "I was too busy preparing to practice." But you can't prepare for trial advocacy only by reading, thinking, and writing. You've got to stand up on your feet and practice speaking.

Practice solo, at least at the beginning. Practicing alone, away from the critical eyes and ears of peers, colleagues, or spouses, provides an opportunity to make mistakes in private. It is nearly impossible to say anything well on the first attempt. Everyone needs multiple tries to express ideas well. Solitary practice gives you a chance to rough draft out loud, get ideas flowing, and take risks and make errors when nobody is watching.

Practice must be out loud. The muscles engaged in the motor skill of talking need exercise, just as those involved with breathing and speaking require warming up, blood flow, and conditioning through repetition. Your entire body needs to practice standing still while talking and gesturing. Practice that simulates as closely as possible the way you will speak out loud in the courtroom should be your goal.

And you should practice a lot—as much as you can. Even busy students or professionals can find 10-or 20-minute blocks of time to rehearse. In addition to such individual practice sessions, stage mock trials with colleagues. All practice serves to improve performance.

You must practice alone, aloud and—ideally—a lot, in order to move ideas that you have read, considered, and written about from inside your head (your neo-cortex) to the tip of your tongue (your articulators). Persuasive advocacy is a motor skill.

To Know and Know How

There is a critical gap between your brain's capacity to *know* something and your body's ability to *know how* to do it physically. Practice bridges that gap. What your brain knows and understands, your body must practice to execute well. An example: suppose you wish to become an expert downhill skier. You read the best book available on the techniques required. Suppose, too, that you're blessed with a photographic memory and are able to remember every technique described in the book. By the time you've finished reading the book, your brain *knows* a great deal about skiing. But such *knowing* doesn't mean that your body possesses the *know-how* to tear down a black diamond run. You have to practice what you learned in your reading to develop the physical know-how necessary to swoosh down a mountain like the ski patrol at Telluride. Your body's muscles, controlled by your motor cortex, need to *get the feel* of the required actions.

This chapter will help you practice to develop advocacy know-how. It will help you get the feel of it. To see the results you're hoping for, you *must* practice—because it is your brain that has read this book, not your body. Your body hasn't a clue about the meaning of the words and ideas in this text.

Trial lawyers used to have more opportunities to develop the know-how of trial advocacy than they do today. In the past, when small cases more often went to trial, advocates could learn the skills of advocacy through experience in the courtroom. For many attorneys in the 21st century, opportunities for on-the-job training no longer exist. Unless you are a prosecutor or a public defender, it is difficult to develop basic trial skills through actual work in real courtrooms. Given the risks of taking a case to trial today, cases are often too important to be entrusted to beginners. But if you lack frequent opportunities to refine and polish your trial skills in actual trials, you have all the more reason to practice those skills, so that you'll be ready when the opportunity to take a case to trial comes along.

The lack of real trial opportunities has led to an increasing number of trial skills training programs for practicing attorneys as well as law students. Participants in such programs, especially busy practitioners, frequently complain that they haven't had enough time to completely digest and assimilate the facts in the case file. They're right. And practice—alone and aloud—is the only way to overcome this problem. When you live with a real case over time, you discuss the case with the client, witnesses, colleagues, opposing counsel, judges, in depositions, etc. You have lots of real-life opportunities to say the facts aloud before presenting the case to a jury. In the training environment, that out-loud experience is missing. Although you have studied the case file, chances are that you have never spoken it. Once you overcome any resistance to practicing alone, aloud, and a lot, you can jump-start your ability to remember the facts of your case and to speak them confidently, even if you've had little time to prepare.

Practice: Resistance and Avoidance

It's unfortunate that "practice makes perfect" sets an impossible expectation. Forget perfection! Your goal in practicing is not to make yourself perfect but to make yourself better—a more sensible and achievable goal. Perfection as an advocate is not only out of reach; it isn't even desirable. The jury doesn't want you to be perfect; they want you to be human, with all the forgivable foibles and imperfections that implies. Your humanity makes you credible.

Don't Use a Mirror

Another reason you may avoid practicing is the suggestion, almost ubiquitous in public speaking training, that you practice in front of a mirror. Pardon this heretical observation, but practicing in front of a mirror is, for most people, a really bad idea! The most important reason to practice is to shed your self-consciousness. Mirrors exist precisely to make the viewer self-conscious. You look in a mirror to make your "self" conscious of your hair, clothing, or makeup. Practicing in front of a mirror raises your self-consciousness, yet the very purpose of practice is to reduce it. The last thing you want is to stand in a courtroom and be overly self-conscious. Your goal is to be conscious of your jury or witness, and fully aware of the situation in the courtroom in all its complexity.

Practicing advocacy skills requires that you rehearse talking to other people, not to yourself. That is virtually impossible if you are staring at yourself in a mirror. After all, who is never going to be called to sit in your jury or be a witness in your case? You! There is no good reason to develop the skill of talking to yourself. You will not be able to monitor your physical behavior, because when you talk to yourself in the mirror you don't engage in the behaviors that you manifest when speaking with others—the very actions you're supposedly trying to see and control. (Later in this chapter, there are two exceptions to the injunction against practicing with a mirror.)

Rationalizations that Inhibit Practicing

"I'm not an actor!"

Some diffident people feel that practicing aloud is synonymous with artifice, pretending, and fakery. Uncomfortable with the self-awareness that practice requires, they worry that their personal integrity and authenticity may somehow be violated. Often they declare, "I'm not an actor! I just can't fake it."

If you are in this group, take a leap of faith. Practicing doesn't make you phony or insincere. Practice will help you find your natural and authentic self when the pressure is on. Once you practice a skill, it becomes second nature. You will have practiced it enough that it feels, appears, and is natural. But it wasn't at first—not until practice made it second nature.

"If this were a real case…"

In training programs, some advocates declare that they are simply too real to practice. This rationalization often begins with the phrase, "Now if this were a real case…" The reality of the case and the trial would supposedly inspire these people to perform well. Yet when asked for some evidence of this theoretical effectiveness, they can't make good on their own prediction. One imagines such people betting their money on athletes who are too real to practice, waiting for the real game to prove their mettle.

"I don't want to be overprepared."

Another frequently heard rationalization for avoiding practice is, "I don't want to be overprepared." What this usually means is that the advocate tried to practice for a short period of time, felt uncomfortable, and quit—and then rationalized quitting as a fear of being overprepared. With a skill as complex as litigation, the odds of your being overprepared are less than the odds of your being struck by lightning during your underprepared opening statement, in the midst of which you may wish, in fact, to be struck by lightning—to end your suffering.

"I feel so silly."

There is one very real emotional challenge regarding practicing. Talking aloud in a room alone is typically taken as a sign of madness! It makes everyone feel, initially, a bit silly, and that feeling may be compounded by the unwarranted fear that someone is listening just outside the door. Frankly, the only solution to this problem is to get over it. Would you rather feel silly in private or in public? Would you rather feel a bit silly—temporarily—talking aloud in a room alone, or feel infinitely more foolish struggling in front of clients and peers in real life?

Since the case ultimately is your client's case and not yours, how do you suppose your client would answer if you were to ask: Should I practice or not? If you yourself were ever a party in a lawsuit, which kind of lawyer would you prefer: the one who is unable or unwilling to practice because she feels silly, or the one who comes into court fully prepared to fight for your cause?

Be Patient

Given how complicated these skills are, be gentle, and generous with yourself as you practice. Be patient. The substantive challenge alone is enormous, and in addition you must also understand the issues of style you will use deliver that substance. It will take time to assimilate and coordinate the necessary knowledge. Your progress will be gradual. The progression of steps in skill acquisition range from beginner to novice, to competent, then proficient, and finally, expert. If you are a beginner, it will take you time, experience, and diligent practice to develop the skills to become a novice, then competent, and finally, proficient. To become expert is an arduous process, but one well worth pursuing.

Persistence

Coaching an experienced intellectual property litigator on his opening statement, Brian Johnson asks him to practice multi-tasking. "Concentrate on eliminating thinking noises," he urges, "and gesture consciously by placing 'on the shelf' the three steps of a conflicts check." He gamely tries, but afterward confesses, "I don't think I did any better that time. In fact, because I was distracted thinking about my gestures, I thought I actually said it worse! And there were still *ums*." He was correct. Practice requires patience and repetition.

On second attempt he does better. His gestures now flow across "the shelf." Having practiced what he wanted to say, he turns his attention to eliminating thinking noises. It still isn't perfect—but practice doesn't make perfect; it makes *better*.

Remember: Practice is a patient progression toward improvement.

How to Practice Step-by-Step

When you stand up in a room alone to practice speaking aloud, your goal is to use, develop, and refine the cognitive skill of structured improvisation. Remember: you will not practice the skill of reading aloud a text you have previously written; you will not practice reciting words that you have memorized; you will not practice in order to memorize your presentation word-for-word so that you can eventually recite it from memory. You will practice extemporaneous speech. You will practice giving your brain an opportunity to process thoughts into words in much the same way you do in everyday conversation, but with one enormous difference: you must be able to think and speak for much longer periods of time, strategically structuring your ideas while obeying the many rules of courtroom procedure governing what you can say and how you can say it.

Practice in order to use the same structure, but not the same words, each time. The structure remains the same; the words are improvised. The exact words will change each time. Your brain already is good at it; now trust that you can do it for longer periods of time in the courtroom.

Before you stand up to talk, create notes so you can practice using them. They should provide a structure for your presentation in outline or bullet point format. Review Chapter Two for suggestions about creating the most effective notes.

Set up your practice room to simulate a courtroom. If you're practicing making an opening statement or closing argument, specify an area across the room where the imaginary jury is seated. Place two chairs far apart enough to indicate the right and left ends of the jury box. Practice speaking to the imaginary jurors. When you practice an examination, place an empty chair across the room to mark the location of the witness stand. Your eyes need a target to focus on, so treat the chair as if a witness were seated there. Focusing your eyes will help focus your brain.

Practice in the Courtroom

If possible, get permission to practice in the actual courtroom where you will conduct your trial. Ask a court official if you can gain access to the courtroom. Speak from the well of the courtroom and fill the room with your voice. Take the witness stand and see that perspective. Sit in the jury box. Bring your visual aids and make certain they are readable by the jury.

Helpful hint: The more you get the feel for a space, the more comfortable you will be.

Run Your Body's Checklist

In your practice room, close the door and get conscious control of your body before you start your practice session. Run your physical checklist, starting with your feet as foundation and moving up the body. The more you practice running this checklist, the more automatic it becomes. Eventually your body will align itself before you speak. Use the checklist from Chapter One and incorporate these extra instructions to refine your preparation ritual.

☐	Eyes	Focus your eyes on the imaginary jury or witness.
☐	Face	Relax the muscles between your eyebrows. Separate your lips slightly.
☐	Head	From the top of your head, gently pull your whole spine upward.
☐	Neck	Lengthen your neck.
☐	Shoulders	Drop your shoulders; let your shoulder blades float down your back.
☐	Hands	Place your hands in the ready position.
☐	Arms	Prepare to gesture; visualize your first gestures.
☐	Breath	Take a few deep, abdominal breaths.
☐	Hips	Center your hips over your feet.
☐	Knees	Unlock your knees.
☐	Feet	Plant your feet and stand still.

Warm Up Your Voice

Chapter Three suggested a routine to help you get reacquainted with your vocal apparatus. Use that routine as your warm-up. Here's a recap:

Stretch your face very wide and stick out your tongue. Then withdraw your tongue and compress all the facial muscles. Stretch and compress these muscles a few times until you can feel the increased blood flow warming your facial muscles.

Repeat these vocal exercises and tongue twisters, over-articulating and increasing your speed as you go:

niminy piminy, niminy piminy, niminy piminy, niminy piminy (etc.)

butta gutta, butta gutta, butta gutta, butta gutta, butta gutta, butta gutta (etc.)

She sells seashells by the seashore.

Three free thugs set three thugs free.

Who What When Where Why Which How (etc.)

Speak in Phrases

Begin speaking at a pace that immediately captures the deliberate rhythm of speaking in phrases. Imitate the rhythm of the *Pledge of Allegiance*. Carefully construct your sentences or questions one phrase at a time to give your brain a chance to collaborate with your speaking voice.

If you must begin with a ritual introduction—"May it please the court, your honor, counsel, members of the jury, my name is…"—use that introductory boilerplate to set a controlled and deliberate pace. Don't rush through it.

Gesture Immediately

Open your gestures just before the very first word comes out of your mouth. The flow of your gestures will lubricate the flow of your thoughts and words. If you are practicing an examination, gesture immediately toward the witness stand using the palm-up, questioning gesture, with one or both hands extended toward your imaginary witness. If you are practicing an opening statement or closing argument, place some initial key words "on the shelf" at waist height.

Talk First and Write Second

Try talking first and writing second. Let the speech center of your brain generate what you intend to say. Once you've said it, write it down, rather than writing first and forcing your brain's speech center to follow the dictates of its writing center. As you rough draft aloud, stop and jot down the ideas you like best. If you like a particular turn of phrase, add it to your notes so that you can decide later whether to keep it for your final presentation. It can be useful just to free-associate aloud as you begin to shape an opening statement or closing argument.

Rough draft aloud what you intend to say; expect it to be uneven and unpolished at first. There is an advantage to finding out what you do not want to say. As with writing, you can go back over the draft and keep polishing.

Practice Your Beginning

Given the rule of primacy, pay particular attention to the beginning of our practice topic. Don't waste your time thanking the jury for their service or offering overdone clichés: "This is the opening statement, which is like a roadmap…" Avoid meaningless filler: "Mr. Harvey, I've just got a few questions…" Practice saying something of interest right at the start, and say it an interesting way. Cut to the chase. Have a dynamic purpose from the very beginning. Start with something that will make the jury want to pay further attention. This is as much a matter of sounding as if you have an interesting purpose as it is of actually having one.

Practice Your Ending

Always end strong, both substantively and stylistically, to follow the rule of recency. Practice it several times until you are confident that it will put a strong finish on your presentation. Make sure to practice what you will ask for in the final paragraph of your opening ("At the end of this trial I will ask you...") or closing argument ("Members of the jury as you deliberate, I ask you to..."). If you genuinely feel the need to thank your jurors for their service, do it in the penultimate position: "Before I conclude, members of the jury, I want to thank you..." An easy way to signal you are nearly done, this guarantees that the jury will attend closely to your conclusion.

Similarly, in examinations, practice the line of questioning that will end your examination. Know and practice your last question in particular. If you haven't planned and practiced your final question, how will you know when your examination is finished? On cross-examination, if you have a zinger for a final question, practice setting it up with the phrase, "Just one final question, Mr. Andersen..." so the jurors are alerted that the end is near. The rule of recency says they are likely to remember what you say just before sitting down, so end with something interesting and memorable that advances your case.

(Do not, of course, practice asking the infamous "one question too many" that opens the door to a detailed refutation of your question by the witness. Practicing the last cross questions aloud will help you hear that potential hazardous question.)

Practice Transitions and Headlines

As a separate memory exercise, say aloud the transitions that will move you from topic to topic. The muscle memory of practicing these transitions aloud will help you remember them under pressure. You may choose sometimes to close out a previous topic definitively before announcing the next one, using recency and primacy as a memory aid and attention-grabber for the jury:

> We have discussed what happened on July 15th.
> *[an ending: where you've been].*
> Now let's focus on the events of July 17th.
> *[a new beginning: where you're going].*

In a direct examination you can use the same technique to help your witness and your jury understand your structure:

> Ms. Wang, we have discussed your educational background *[ending]*;
> now let's talk about your professional experience *[beginning].*

If you remind the jury and the witness where you've been, and tell them where you're going next, they're more likely to know where you are, and to stay with you in the present moment.

During cross-examination you usually will be cagier about your structure, to avoid tipping off the witness about where you're going. Therefore, practice the transition from one line of questioning to the next, without the obvious recency/primacy, ending/beginning headlines of direct examination. If, before moving on, you want the jury to think about your previous line of questioning, practice inserting persuasive silence as you transition to the next topic. During this silence you are subliminally suggesting to the jury, "Think about that!" Count to yourself two or three seconds of silence to let your jury think about what the witness just admitted. Let them realize the importance of your previous line of questioning, then move on. Three seconds will feel like a long time, but of course it isn't. If you practice counting the seconds silently, you'll begin to get comfortable with using longer silences for transitions.

Practice Jump-Starting Your Gestures

Practice how you will jump-start your instinct to gesture so that it immediately takes over, freeing you to think about more important things. Decide exactly what you want to say, and then find a gesture appropriate to your words. Place key words "on the shelf." Your emphasis will be reinforced by accompanying gestures at waist height.

For example, in opening statement it's logical to gesture as you state your theme: "This is a case about personal responsibility." Emphasize *case* with one hand "on the shelf" and *personal responsibility* with the other hand.

A direct examination may begin by instructing your witness: "Please introduce yourself to the members of the jury." Gesture logically with one hand toward the witness as you say *yourself* and with the other hand, gesture toward the members of *the jury*, directing the witness to address them.

Suppose your cross-examination of the arson expert begins with the leading question, "Mr. Harris, isn't it a fact that you never went to the scene of the fire?" That question could be delivered with both hands directed toward the witness, doing the palms-up questioning gesture to emphasize the words *fact* or *never* (or both!). (To control the witness physically and insist on his answering, keep your hands in the extended position until he begins to speak.)

Or suppose you decide to begin a closing argument by saying, "The defendant didn't *look*, and he didn't *listen*, because he was *distracted*." All three of those key words can be placed "on the shelf," using the double karate-chop gesture to emphasize each one in turn.

When You Must Read Aloud: Practice!

There are times when you need to read from a document in court. You may read from a report, contract, witness statement, or deposition during impeachment. Resist the temptation to read too fast for your listeners to comprehend. When you must read, here's how to do it effectively:

Pick up the document and hold it up. Don't leave it on the lectern.

Read it a phrase at a time, emphasizing key words in each phrase.

Read the meaning of the words, not just the words themselves.

Practice reading aloud slowly and, if you need to, mark up the document to assist your reading. Put slash marks where you intend to pause between phrases, and underline the key words in each phrase that clarify the meaning. A few minutes of mindful practice will ensure that you make the greatest possible impact. Having significant impact is, after all, the point of reading any document aloud. Don't leave that impact to chance.

When You Recite from Memory

Sometimes the verbatim repetition *of a phrase or sentence* will be useful, or even necessary, in trial. You may have to quote your client or an opposing party, or refer to the precise language of a contract, letter, e-mail, statement, transcript, or deposition. In cases like these, practice saying these words until they roll off your tongue easily. Whenever you plan to quote a person or document verbatim, double-check to make sure you have memorized the quotation accurately. It can be very persuasive to be able to quote something precisely from memory during a trial, but you must not paraphrase.

Notes and Visual Aids

Once you have structured and practiced your whole presentation, make sure to practice with the final version of your notes. Write legibly and large enough so that your notes are easy to see, whether placed on a lectern or left on the edge of counsel table.

If you plan to use visual aids in a courtroom presentation, practice working with them. Make sure they're legible from the jury box. Sit as far away from them as your jurors will to check for legibility. If you're going to write on a flip chart, practice writing big, legibly, and carefully. Don't rush. Then step back from your writing and see whether it's readable from a distance. Generally, "jumbo" size marker pens make flip chart visuals vastly easier to read than regular markers. Practice using the flat edge to make the most legible script.

As you practice speaking with your visual aid, stand with your toes pointed toward your imaginary jury. If you point your toes toward the visual aid, you'll end up addressing it instead of the people you want to persuade. Pointing your toes toward the jurors will keep you facing in the right direction. When you gesture to your visual aid, use the arm that is closest to it. When you point to something on the visual aid, leave your hand on the visual aid for reference, but turn your head and eyes back to speak to the jury. Touch the visual, turn to the jury, and then talk to them. Think of these as the 3 Ts: touch, turn, talk.

Practice with computer-generated visual aids on a big screen. This will give you a feel for what the jury will be seeing for the first time. Give them time to absorb what is there. Adjust your pace and rhythm to accommodate your jurors when you want them to read what you've put up on the screen. It is counterproductive to ask jurors to split their focus between listening to you and looking at the screen. Give them time to read. Tell them what they are looking at:

This is the emergency room report.

Tell them where on the screen you want them to look:

Look halfway down the page at the box indicating blood alcohol level.

Don't talk to the screen; talk to the jury about what is on the screen. If you intend to read from a visual aid, practice reading from it with the same deliberate style described above.

When you are finished with a slide, get rid of it by going to a blank slide that will turn your screen blue or black.

Practice Courtroom Rituals Aloud

There are many spoken rituals in the courtroom that require you to say aloud the necessary steps in the proper order, for both the judge and the record. These rituals include the steps to get an exhibit into evidence, or to impeach a witness with a prior inconsistent statement. If you practice these rituals aloud, you will be able to march through the steps with confidence. They should be automatic.

> I am holding what has been pre-marked as Defendant's exhibit #1 for identification.
>
> Showing to opposing counsel…
>
> Your honor, may I approach the witness?
>
> I'm showing you what has been pre-marked as Defendant's exhibit #1 for identification.
>
> [etc., etc., etc.]

Different types of exhibits require different verbal rituals to move them into evidence successfully. Laying the foundation for a photograph is different from laying the foundation for a business record. Practice asking these various foundational questions, in their proper order, until they are automatic. Walk through the steps in your practice space, saying the exact words aloud, as if you were showing the exhibit to opposing counsel and approaching the witness. The more you practice the full routine, actions as well as words, the more your muscle memory will assist you in remembering it under pressure.

Use a Video Camera

There is no feedback more valuable than seeing and hearing yourself as others do. If you have access to a video camera, use it. When you practice with a camera, don't speak directly at the camera with your eyes focused on the lens—it is too difficult to keep your concentration while talking to a machine. If you are using a chair as a witness stand, place the camera slightly off to the side. Or place the camera where the jury will be sitting to see yourself from the jurors' perspective.

When you watch the video, be gentle and generous with yourself. Don't focus only on what you don't like. See and hear the positive elements as well. One way to be more objective and technical in your self-analysis is to attend to the observable, quantifiable elements of persuasive style: How often do you move your feet? How many steps are you taking per minute? How many seconds do you pause to think or let your jury think? How long does it take for you to use your first gesture? How many seconds do your gestures last? Once you know the numbers, you can set clear goals to walk or shift less often, to pause longer, or to gesture sooner the next time you practice. A video review checklist in Appendix 2 will help you evaluate yourself.

When to Use a Mirror

Practicing with a mirror can make you self-conscious as you gaze at your own face. Here is a suggestion for using a mirror. Tape a piece of paper on the mirror so that it obscures your face, but leaves the rest of your body visible. You are now the "headless advocate." This painless self-decapitation allows you to focus on the rest of your body, and especially on your gestures. As you practice aloud, notice if your gestures are too small or too fast. The mirror provides immediate feedback without making you excessively self-conscious.

When you choose an attitude, mirrors can be helpful. Look at your face in the mirror and play with different attitudes to get a feel for them. Because attitude is reflected in demeanor, the mirror can help you refine your performance.

Exercises to Solve Specific Problems

"I talk too softly."

If you talk too softly, practice taking deeper, abdominal breaths both before and while you are speaking. Slow your pace deliberately to give yourself time to draw in longer, larger breaths between sentences. Practice speaking a sentence at a time, stopping to take a deeper breath at the ends of sentences. Because emphatic words are louder, emphasize at least one key word in every phrase.

Soft-spoken people tend to trail off on the final phrase or word of a sentence or question. To counter this tendency, speak more loudly as you approach the ends of sentences or questions. Deliberately stress the final word of each sentence. Tell yourself to be louder at the end of the sentence. This will keep the volume consistent throughout the utterance.

"I just can't stand still."

Stand up and consciously feel the soles of your feet inside your shoes. Wiggle your toes. Feel your feet in contact with the floor, which sits upon the foundation of the building, which is planted on the earth. Your pedestal is the whole planet; feel yourself anchored to it. Do not move your feet as you start to talk. Inhibit the instinct to talk and walk simultaneously. Keep your feet planted as you begin to speak, and let your arms do the walking.

Gesture immediately. Physical energy naturally seeks release downward, into your legs. Instead, send it into your arms, which also will make it apparent in your voice. At first, practice saying only a single paragraph or topic without moving your feet, then gradually work up to doing an entire opening or closing standing in one place. Once you can stand still, practice using a limited number of moves. During an opening, for example, stand in one place to talk about your client, and then move to a different location to discuss the opposing party. Shift a third time to conclude. Practice using a limited number of moves for transitions between topics in examinations.

"I speak too quickly."

Speaking too quickly is merely a habit, and habits can be broken. Practice speaking in phrases while attending to the short silences separating your phrases and sentences. Before you speak, take a deep breath and concentrate on hearing the silence in the room. When you speak, exploit this silence. Begin speaking, and immediately insert silence between your first phrases. When you come to the end of a sentence, stop for a longer span of time than your instincts might dictate. Imagine that the period at the end of the sentence is a stoplight, and that you plan to sit silently at that stoplight for a short while. Focus less on the speed at which you are talking than on the gaps between phrases when you are *not* talking.

To discover a suitable rhythm, say aloud the phrases below. Hear the silence before and between the phrases:

> *(Hear the silence in the room as you inhale)*
> Your only goal *(hear the silence)*
> is to control the pace *(hear the silence)*
> by using silence *(hear the silence)*
> intentionally inserted *(hear the silence)*
> between phrases and sentences *(hear the silence).*

Use that pace as you practice all phases of trial. Once you can hear the silence, notice how much easier it is to speak when you give yourself time to think. Simply shorten the silent gaps between phrases and sentences until you find the appropriate pace for speaking in the courtroom. This is an exercise, not an attempt to find a realistic courtroom pace. Once you know how to slow yourself down, you can pick up the tempo again.

"My eyes aren't focused."

Make it your ritual to focus first and talk second. Don't speak until your gaze is fixed on an imaginary witness, judge, or jury across the room. Then speak aloud as you continue to intentionally focus your eyes. When you find your eyes wandering, perhaps looking toward the floor or ceiling as you pause to think, be aware of breaking eye contact and return to your original point of focus. Look directly at your imaginary witness as you practice asking questions of him. Draw a life-size pair of eyes on a piece of paper and tape the "eyes" to the chair. Focus on them as you ask questions. Identify the area where your imaginary jury is sitting, and speak to them. Use a couple of chairs to indicate the ends of the jury box; then, as you speak, make roving eye contact with the imaginary individual jurors seated within that perimeter.

"I say *um* too much."

To eliminate the *um* habit, substitute silence in its place. Choose a topic that's familiar and ordinary, and begin talking. Describe what you did last weekend. Talk about what you did on your last vacation. Speak at full voice; don't mumble. As you talk aloud, your only goals are to speak in phrases and to mind the gaps between phrases and sentences. The pace isn't important, the silence is. Your aim is to activate your awareness of thinking noises and the silences that will replace them.

Before you begin, hear the silence around you. Start talking, and insert silence into the gaps between phrases and sentences. Here is a typographical example of the pace:

Last weekend… *(mind the gap)*
I was extremely busy…*(mind the gap)*
and I didn't stop for a minute. *(mind the gap)*
When I awoke on Saturday…*(mind the gap)*
the first thing I needed to do…*(mind the gap)*
was to run some errands…*(mind the gap)*
and get my oil changed. *(mind the gap)*

Go as slowly as you must in order to keep the silence in the gaps. Start to hear when you use a thinking noise, and then begin to hear the preferable, silent alternative.

When you use a thinking noise, hear it and take note of it, but don't stop to chastise yourself. Such a deeply ingrained, persistent habit will continue to appear periodically. Continue speaking, with your goal being to speak for longer and longer stretches without using a thinking noise. When you hear one, be aware of it, and avoid using it as you go forward.

Once you have free-associated about last weekend or your vacation, repeat this exercise but speak about a topic related to the law. Use one that is currently on your mind or on your desk. Explain something legal. Talk about what "beyond a reasonable doubt" or "preponderance of the evidence" means. Explain the difference between a trademark and a copyright. Imagine yourself teaching a non-lawyer the meaning of a legal concept or term—just as you will need to teach a jury during a trial. Again, the subject of your talk is less important than your awareness of minding the gaps between phrases.

Keep your practice sessions short; initially, just five to ten minutes is best. Gradually, lengthen the time you are able to speak with articulate control and without thinking noises. Practice longer presentations, such as an opening or closing. Once you have developed sufficient awareness, the next step is to practice conversation without thinking noises. Use silence instead of *um* in more casual settings. The more you do this, the sooner you'll develop a new habit: the habit of speaking without thinking noises. Once you can do this outside the courtroom, it is relatively easy to be articulate when you stand up in court.

Your goal is to be able to turn off the thinking noises whenever it matters. In everyday conversation, the *ums* and *uhs* simply aren't important. Sitting at your kitchen table, talking with a friend in a restaurant, conversing with a colleague at the water cooler—who cares if you say *um* then? You should care, however, about eliminating thinking noises when you are communicating professionally. Whether talking to a colleague or client, in person or on the phone, you should be able to be completely fluent and articulate. Practice in your simulated courtroom, your car, or on the phone.

"I say *okay* after answers on direct examination."

Many lawyers unconsciously say *okay* after a witness gives an answer during direct examination. Like all habits, this reflexive use of *okay* is difficult to break, and for several reasons. *Okay* is the expression we use in conversation to affirm that we are listening and understanding. We nod; we say *uh-huh, mmmmmm,* or *okay.* Practitioners unconsciously reinforce this habit by saying *okay* repeatedly while taking depositions.

You can't eliminate this habit by giving yourself the negative instruction: "Stop saying *okay!*" Your brain does not respond well to these admonitions, especially when it's unaware of inserting *okay* in the first place. If you were aware of saying it, you would stop. Rather than trying to attack this habit directly, examine your timing—on when you say *okay.* It happens immediately after your witness finishes an answer. *Okay* pops out of your mouth before you have time to monitor it, much less eliminate it. It sounds like this:

Q: What do you do for a living?
A: I'm a plumber.
Q: *Okay...* How long have you been a plumber?
A: Twenty years.
Q: *Okay...* Who do you work for?
A: Myself.
Q: *Okay...*

Since *okay* happens right after the answer, focus your attention on that moment. As soon as the witness finishes speaking, inhale. *Okay* cannot slip out while a breath is slipping in. It takes about one second to fill your lungs with air, the same amount of time it takes to say *okay.* During that time, let your jury think about the witness' answer while you formulate your next question. As you inhale, think of the first word of your next question. It is not *okay,* but rather *who, what, when, where, why, which, how, describe, explain,* or *tell.*

Practice your direct examination aloud, addressing the witness chair in your imaginary courtroom. Inhale intentionally before each question. Train your body to inhale reflexively after the witness finishes an answer. This new habit (*inhale!*) will displace the old habit (*okay*). Try playing both roles in your practice session: ask the question, and then provide the answer you think the witness will give. Between the answer and your next question, consciously inhale. You'll know you are making progress when your lips form the word *okay,* but you catch yourself before it pops out. Be ready to stop yourself when you reach that stage.

"I begin leading questions with *And...* on cross-examination."

Leading questions on cross-examination often begin with the conjunction: *And...* which is then sometimes followed by a thinking noise: *And...uh...* This is a common verbal habit, similar to saying *okay* during direct examination. The word *and* slips out before the advocate is even aware of it, much less able to suppress it:

Q: You are a plumber, right?
A: Yes.
Q: *And...*you've been a plumber for 20 years, true?
A: Yes.
Q: *And...uh...* you work for yourself?
A: Yes.
Q: *And...uh...*

In natural conversation, we frequently link sentences with the conjunction *and.* It is a common, deeply ingrained verbal habit, which is why your brain is primed to insert *and* between questions on cross-examination. As with other habits, you can't eliminate this habit by giving yourself the negative instruction: "Don't say *AND!*" Give yourself a positive instruction. Just as with *okay,* substitute a conscious breath.

You say *and* or *and uh* immediately after your witness has answered your question. As soon as the witness finishes the answer, inhale! *And* cannot slip out while the breath is slipping in.

Practice saying aloud the leading questions in your cross-examination. Consciously inhale before asking each question, training your body to inhale reflexively before each question. Play both roles and answer your own question aloud. After you have answered yes or no, inhale before asking the next question.

"I'm so boring."

Tackle this problem in two ways. If possible, watch yourself on video. Evaluate whether your face is a mask of seriousness, your demeanor is grim, or both. First, fix your face. Alter your brow, eyes, and lips to achieve neutral alert, as discussed in Chapter One. If your brow is furrowed, relax it. Raise your eyebrows, and part your lips.

Now, ask yourself what your face tells the listener. Are you curious? Impatient? Detached? The default courtroom attitude is austere, solemn, and somber; something that could be described as Courtroom Gothic, or simply, Dead on Arrival. Unrelenting austerity is rarely a compelling or interesting human attitude. While almost everything in a courtroom is weighty, of course, a monochromatic long-faced demeanor quickly wears out its welcome. While always staying within the limits of what is appropriate, choose an attitude as a tactical choice. Refer to the list of attitudes in Chapter Two to re-energize your demeanor. Pick an attitude to suit your tactics.

Appealing to the Jury

After repeatedly practicing a short appeal for donations to a nonprofit's capital campaign, a volunteer asked for a critique from his committee. "Your attitude is too stern," was the response. "It feels like a reprimand rather than an appeal for money." There was nothing appealing about his demeanor.

To appeal to your jury, sometimes you should be friendly. If you want the jury to agree with you, be agreeable. Righteous indignation, properly directed at your opposition, can feel unpleasant and off-putting when directed at your jury. Their response is likely to be, "Don't yell at us, counsel, we didn't do it!" The medium is the message.

Lesson learned: Once you decide what you want to say, practice saying it with a persuasive attitude appropriate for the situation.

One simple way to find a more interesting attitude is to ask this question: What is the feeling or attitude you wish to provoke in the jury? In opening statement, use one attitude when you talk about your client and another when you talk about the opposing party. In a serious personal injury case you would use one attitude to describe how great life was for your client before the accident: "He used to run five miles every day." Use a different attitude to describe how grim life has become since the accident: "Now he can't stand up without help." On direct examination, practice curiosity—let the jury know your witness is interesting. If you want the jury to feel skeptical about a witness on cross, adopt skepticism. Or kill the witness with kindness, at least at the beginning, and get tough later on. Practice your closing argument, adopting specific attitudes: plead, beg, and cajole the jury with your arguments. Be indignant, surprised, hostile, wistful, nostalgic, sarcastic.

The Boundary of "Too Much"

An attorney comes for a video review saying, "I tried to stretch myself. I took a big risk and felt I was overdoing it. At one point I got so loud I was yelling." Watching his performance he says, "It doesn't sound nearly as dramatic as it felt. What felt like yelling was only a little louder. I was not overdoing it at all." Why is this a common response in video review?

While performing, your self-awareness is heightened. Heightened awareness seems to magnify the choices you are making—but only in your self-perception. What feels like "yelling," however, is only slightly louder than your normal voice. What feels like a huge gesture is only slightly bigger than usual; that "long pause" is really only three seconds. In order to get it just right, practice what feels like too much.

Helpful hint: The boundary of "too much" is much farther away than you think.

Informal Practice Sessions

The various practice sessions suggested above are all relatively formal. When you stand up in a room alone to practice aloud, you simulate the reality of the courtroom. These practice sessions are essential, but they are by no means your only opportunities to practice. You can also create informal practice sessions to improve your skills. These informal sessions don't allow you to practice every skill simultaneously, but they can be very useful for coordinating your brain and speaking voice. Here are some suggestions for informal practice:

1. Practice speaking aloud while driving in your car. Although you shouldn't practice gesturing when behind the wheel, drive time offers a good opportunity to practice such verbal skills as eliminating thinking noises, speaking too quickly, or speaking too softly. Look at the clock on the dashboard and make yourself practice for a set amount of time—say, ten minutes. Be uninhibited. If you are driving to court for a trial, this kind of practice is especially valuable; it serves as your verbal warm-up. Your self-confidence will be much greater if you can stand up in court thinking, "I've already said this aloud many times as I drove here today."

2. Practice speaking aloud while walking for exercise. You'll be in good company: Abraham Lincoln practiced this way. According to historian Harold Holzer, "To familiarize himself with the speech, he took to reciting passages aloud as he walked down the streets of Springfield…" This is a good time to rough draft aloud your opening statement or closing argument. Start by practicing discrete moments, such as the first or the final paragraph of your opening or closing. Test out alternative themes this way.

3. Practice speaking aloud during your morning ablutions on days when you must speak in court. As you shower or make coffee, practice saying aloud what you must say under pressure later that day. Hours before you must speak under pressure, give your brain and voice a chance to get warmed up and coordinated. This type of practice develops muscle memory, which is extremely helpful. When possible, practice speaking aloud right before you have to perform. Step into a nearby empty room, a deserted stairwell, or even an unoccupied restroom, and say your first sentences aloud. You will be primed and ready to go.

Practice During Everyday Conversations

Every time you speak, you have an opportunity to be articulate and understandable. It is especially easy and useful to practice when you aren't feeling the pressure to perform. In casual chats with friends and colleagues, practice eliminating thinking noises. In personal conversations, slow down your pace and speak in phrases. In meetings or classes, push yourself to ask a question or volunteer an observation as a brief test of your speaking skills under pressure.

To prepare for the challenge of direct examination, ask open-ended questions in conversation. Ask questions that begin with *who, what, when, where, why, which, how, describe, explain,* or *tell.* Not only will you be a more engaging conversational partner, you will also develop the ability to draw information out of another person while directing the conversation—a crucial skill in direct examination.

Observe, Adapt, and Adopt

Steal ideas from good role models. Adapt or adopt some of the elements of their style and make them your own. When you hear truly excellent speakers, look and listen closely to understand why they make such a strong impression. Listen to their pacing. How much do they use silence? Watch their eyes. Look at their gestures. Could you adapt a particularly effective gesture and make it your own? Expanding your gestural vocabulary is like expanding your verbal vocabulary; just as you can learn a new word and use it tellingly, you can learn a new gesture and make it part of your personal style.

When you hear mediocre speakers, ask yourself why they make a poor impression. Count the thinking noises. Determine if the pace is too fast. Note those elements of style that you want to avoid in your own delivery, and practice doing the opposite.

The Law of Opposites

As you hone your style, become aware of its individual elements. Perhaps you speak with volume and authority, and are an articulate but fast talker. You gesture regularly as part of emphasizing key words. Simply put, you are loud, fast, and animated. These are all good things to have as elements of your personal style, but it is possible to have too much of a good thing. Contrast and variety will best be achieved if you tell yourself periodically that in addition to being loud, fast, and animated, you can also be softer, slower, and still. Invoke the law of opposites, and force your loud voice to be sometimes softer, your fast delivery slower, and your animated gestures still.

When you obey the law of opposites, you suddenly have twice as many skills to call upon. Rather than just playing to your strengths—loud, fast, animated—you also play against them. This keeps your delivery interesting. The jury then anticipates the next surprise and contrast, rather than feeling perpetually barraged by the same stylistic elements. Human beings crave variety. We quickly tire of the same old thing repeated over and over again. This is especially true of style. Surprise your jury and mix up your choices to keep your voice and presentation from becoming predictable, repetitive, and ultimately, boring.

When you go in an unexpected stylistic direction, you gain a new expressive capacity. The power of the unobvious choice—of doing what the jury has not foreseen—is its ability to mark important words, phrases, sentences, and questions. If your style is loud, fast, and animated, you can't very well highlight important points by being even louder, faster, and more animated. That would be too much! Instead, choose from a broader range of stylistic elements. Ask yourself "What is the opposite of my usual demeanor?" Add an exotic spice to a favorite recipe. You need just a dash of soft, slow, and still, not a personality transplant or a radical change of delivery.

Practice making such uncharacteristic choices before trying this technique under pressure in court. With practice, you will find that your stylistic vocabulary has widened and that you can make the novel choice spontaneously. Like a skilled jazz musician, you will eventually live in the present and feel the moment when a choice is instinctively right.

Practicing for the Mental Game

Finding your rituals, developing a solid technique, and relying on good speaking habits all go a long way towards helping you feel prepared to walk into the courtroom. Psyching yourself up for trial, rather than psyching yourself out, is one last critical part of your technique. You have to successfully play the "head game" with yourself to anticipate and look forward to the pressure of performing as an advocate. Mental preparation for trial is as much a matter of technique and practice as eliminating thinking noises or learning to stand still. Each lawyer has unique challenges in getting ready. Here are some ways to think about how to practice for the mental game.

Litigators engage in a competitive battle of wits. There is a winner, a loser, and a judge as referee. To play to win, psych yourself up before competing, just as athletes do. Athletes chant, shout, and supportively slap each other to get psyched up. Pump yourself up as part of your technique: "I can do this! I can win." Confidence is based on preparation. Tell yourself, "I'm ready. I practiced. I've done everything I can to prepare for this trial. Now, I want to win." Use the techniques in this book to be prepared. Then, you can psyche yourself up, not out.

If you have ever had a really unpleasant speaking experience, you may suffer from PTSD or "post-traumatic speaking disorder." Perhaps you blanked while speaking to your peers in law school, college, or even earlier in your life. Does that one bad experience haunt you still? Time to get over it.

Make a video while practicing and review it using the Video Review Checklist in the Appendix. Watch and listen, focusing on the positive elements of style. On a piece of paper, tally the things you already do that work well. Be specific: "I stand still. I don't say *um*. I gesture naturally. I don't appear nervous." Build your newfound confidence on that foundation. Don't be overly critical of the things you don't like. The next time you have to perform, study that list of positive things, and tell yourself, "Here's what I do that works." Focus on those positive elements of your style – and you will gradually overcome PTSD, putting it behind you forever.

Trial work can trigger deeply personal issues and anxieties. Some lawyers confess they hate being the center of attention. Others don't like to be stared at intensely. Still others don't like making eye contact with strangers. Some are uncomfortable mustering the assertiveness required for cross-examination; it feels too aggressive and domineering.

If you are dealing with any of these issues, you can change. Make a conscious decision to work on your personal anxiety. Pinpoint what bothers you the most, practice that specific skill, and get comfortable doing it.

Of all the techniques in this book, the practice of conscious breathing is the most important, but also the most undervalued. As you prepare for a trial, deliberate breathing can help to turn off unhelpful thoughts of negative anticipation. When the bailiff calls, "All rise!" and you know you are about to begin a trial, breathing is the last thing you can do to keep your wits about you. The more you employ this technique, the better it works. If you focus on conscious breathing in the present moment, you won't focus on fretting about the future.

Don't Let 'Em See You Sweat

One common and deeply personal issue lawyers cope with is sweating. Some people, including one author of this book, perspire easily and sometimes copiously. Here are some suggestions for how to cope:

Drink less coffee. Linger in a cool shower. Turn down the air conditioning. Dress and walk with deliberate slowness.

Wear a white shirt, since colored shirts darken visibly with perspiration. Breathe more slowly than usual. Drink water; suck on ice. Arrive early, so you needn't rush. Sit down, breathe deeply and slowly. Buy a tiny battery-operated fan the size of a cell phone and use it. Always have a cotton handkerchief in your pocket, just in case. If your problem is extreme, *Help! I'm Sweating! Causes, Phenomena, Therapies,* by Dietmar Stattkus might be helpful. But don't hesitate to consult your doctor if you feel your predicament warrants medical intervention. There are remedies.

Remember: There are many ways to mitigate sweating. Lots of people experience the problem.

You may sweat, blush, suffer from nerves, or wonder why you ever wanted to put up with the stress of a trial lawyer's life. But you can figure out how to overcome your issues. Nobody was born being a star in the courtroom. Everybody had to learn it. You will, too.

Practice Makes Human

The experienced trial lawyer stands before the panel of prospective jurors for jury selection. With his flowing gray hair and immaculate suit, he looks to be the central casting stereotype of a polished trial lawyer. He turns to the next member of the panel and asks a question that is so convoluted and confusing that the woman simply knits her brow and stares at him in silence. Seeing her expression, he says, "Ms. Slettom, is that the dumbest question you've ever been asked?" The entire panel laughs aloud. "I thought so too," he confesses, "Let me try that again."

His frank acknowledgment of his humanity cemented his

rapport with the panel and the future members of the jury; he ultimately won the case.

Remember: Don't be afraid to be yourself in the courtroom. And being yourself sometimes means you will make mistakes. When it happens, admit it, fix it, and move on.

Summary

Yes, you may feel self-conscious; yes, practicing isn't always easy; yes, bad habits can be stubborn; yes, there are many skills to be learned; yes, one can backslide if one doesn't use those skills; etc. But practice really does work, producing tangible results in a surprisingly short time. Ask any professional athlete or musician. If you've managed to read this far without actually trying any of the exercises suggested, put down the book and give it a whirl.

Practice is the only way to improve any skill. It is the ultimate skill, allowing you to turn what you know into the solid performance skill of know-how. Conquer any resistance you may feel about practicing and learn to do it alone, aloud, and a lot. Remember, you are not prepping yourself to be perfect; you are practicing to get better. Be patient and methodical. It doesn't have to take hours every day. Short sessions may be more productive.

Create notes to serve as a visual aid that will allow you to refine the skill of structured improvisation. As you begin, run up the body's checklist from feet to head. Warm up your articulators so those muscles are ready to work. Give special energy and attention to rehearsing beginnings and endings. Once you decide what you wish to say to begin, train yourself to jump-start your instinct to gesture.

Practice with your visual aids, and if you intend to read from a document, read it numerous times, deliberately and with meaning. If you have a particular skill you are attempting to improve, take ten minutes a day to focus exclusively on that skill.

In addition to formal practice sessions, use speaking opportunities in everyday life—informal practice—to improve your ability to communicate fluently and articulately.

Carefully observe other advocates and public speakers; adopt and adapt the skills you see used by gifted communicators. Understand and avoid those problems that make mediocre speakers less effective.

Birds! Damn it, birds!

Opening night of a stage play is thrilling for the actors. The rehearsal hall has given way to a theater with sets, costumes, and bright lights, and the audience reacts in unexpected, exciting ways. There is applause, the anticipation of reviews to come. Second performances, though, can be a letdown. The adrenaline of opening night has dissipated, and the possibility of a mediocre performance from tired actors is a well-documented pitfall.

A veteran stage director gathered his cast before every second performance for a stern pep talk. "Long ago when I was a young dancer in vaudeville," he would say, "I was in a show that included a flock of dancing flamingos. Their 'dressing room' was a pen in the wings, where they heard everything that happened onstage. When their entrance music played, they began to squawk, flap their wings, and leap in the air with excitement. Those flamingos couldn't wait to get onstage and perform."

Then he paused dramatically, looked at each actor in the cast and said, "Birds! Damn it—*birds* can get up for a performance. So go out there tonight and break a leg!"

Helpful hint: If birds can psych themselves up to perform, so can you.

Trial advocacy is an incredibly complicated game. As in every game, there is a winner and a loser. The judge acts as referee. The rules are complex, and it takes a long time to learn to play well. The game is so fascinating that it is not only our system of justice, it's also a popular spectator sport. Television series, movies, and plays exploit the entertainment value of watching trials. And like any sport, the only way to excel, and be a winner, is to practice.

Mantras of Self-Instruction

- [ ] Breathe consciously.
- [ ] Take larger and longer breaths.
- [ ] Emphasize a key word in every phrase.
- [ ] Be louder at the end of each utterance.
- [ ] Plant your feet and stand still.
- [ ] Feel the floor; wiggle your toes.
- [ ] Anchor yourself.
- [ ] Gesture immediately.
- [ ] Let your arms do the walking.
- [ ] Move for transitions.
- [ ] Hear the silence.
- [ ] Use the silence.
- [ ] Speak in phrases.
- [ ] Make your sentences end.

☐ Linger longer at each period.

☐ Focus first; talk second.

☐ When you break contact, reconnect.

☐ Pause longer at the ends of sentences.

☐ When the answer ends, inhale.

☐ As you breathe in, think: first word.

☐ Attitude is a tactical choice: pick one.

☐ Practice alone, aloud, a lot.

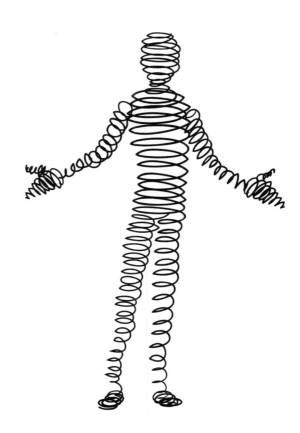

Appendices

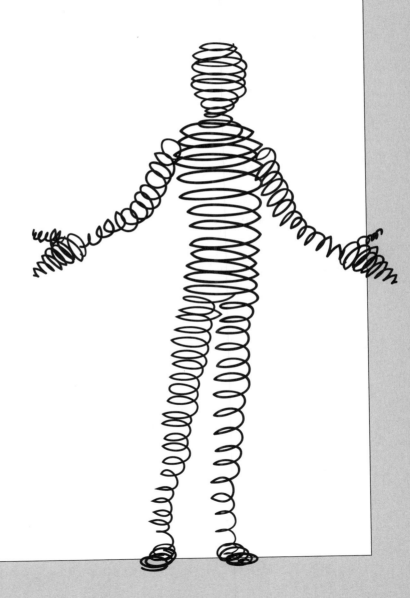

Appendix 1

Speaking Persuasively, Thinking On Your Feet

Coordinating your body, your brain, and your voice for effective advocacy

Controlling Your Body

☐ Before you stand up to speak, get conscious control of your breath by inhaling deeply and exhaling slowly.

☐ Continue to breathe deeply and slowly as you walk to the well of the courtroom.

☐ Relax your facial expression; release any tension from your mouth or eyebrows.

☐ Adopt a dynamic stance: center your weight evenly on both feet. Don't slouch or lean on lecterns or tables.

☐ Make eye contact with all your jurors before you start talking. Systematically look at those seated at the four corners of the jury perimeter.

☐ Look up from your notes and focus on the judge, jury, or witness before you speak. Before you ask your first question, make eye contact with the witness.

☐ Place your hands in a ready position, loosely touching at waist height with elbows bent at 90 degrees.

☐ Get the arms ready to gesture before you speak, then instruct your body to release the gestures as you talk.

☐ Inhale consciously one last time before uttering your first sentence. This breath will support and project your voice. Breathe in, speak out.

☐ Remember the 3 R's of natural gesturing: Ready to gesture, Release gestures, and Relax your arms at your sides occasionally.

☐ Channel the adrenaline created by exhilaration and/or anxiety into big, smooth gestures.

☐ Gestures that are larger in size and longer in duration will make you feel and appear more natural.

☐ Get some "air in the armpits" and your gestures will look and feel more natural. Gesture from the shoulder, not just from the elbow.

☐ Plan and practice an initial trigger gesture to help jump-start your natural instinct to gesture.

☐ Trigger gestures: GIVE (facts or questions), CHOP (emphasis), or SHOW (on the one hand...on the other hand).

☐ Smoothly fill your natural zone of gesture: a rectangular space approximately five feet wide by two feet high.

☐ Gesture with open hands and open palms; don't curl your fingers inward.

☐ When asking questions, use the palms up, questioning gesture.

☐ Once you jump-start your initial gestures, stop thinking about them and let your instinct take over.

Controlling Your Brain

☐ Don't tell yourself to "Relax!" Instead, raise and release your energy level as you begin speaking.

☐ To get your brain focused, talk to people, not paper. Don't look at notes during your opening sentences or questions.

☐ Imagine you are speaking with individuals, not talking to an impersonal, monolithic jury.

☐ Don't be surprised at your jurors' stoic, deadpan facial expressions. (It has nothing to do with you!)

☐ Recognize the time warp created by adrenaline; plan to speak slowly at the start to compensate for your altered perception of time.

☐ Pauses are good; silence is golden. Short pauses give you time to think ahead and jurors time to absorb.

☐ Lay out the structure of your presentation for the jury. Saying it aloud will help you remember it, too.

☐ Reveal your enthusiasm and interest in your case, and be appropriately friendly when possible.

☐ Realize that your jury can't tell how nervous you are inside; take comfort in that realization.

☐ Be patient and don't hit the panic button when you need to mentally search for your next word or idea.

☐ Use headlines to announce new topics during examinations: "Now let's focus on…"

☐ When using notes, less is more! Use only bullet points to trigger bigger thoughts. Resist reading from your notes.

☐ Don't be afraid to look at your notes between topics! Listeners only object when you talk to your notes.

☐ Notes are a visual aid for you, so write big, and keep them simple. Put notes where they are easy to see.

Controlling Your Voice

☐ Breathe deeply and vigorously! The power of your speaking voice is proportional to your breath support.

☐ To control the pace, speak in phrases, not whole sentences. Use the rhythm of the *Pledge of Allegiance*.

☐ Breathe consciously as a witness answers, in order to refill your lungs.

☐ Vary the pace: speak in phrases on important points, and speak more briskly for preliminary information.

☐ Control any unconscious thinking noises—*um* and *uh*—by consciously substituting silence instead.

☐ Emphasis creates meaning, so speak vigorously to stress the key word or phrases in every sentence or question.

☐ Recognize that words deserving emphasis are often at ends of sentences or questions.

☐ Emphasize the endings of your sentences to keep your voice from trailing off.

☐ Beware of the pitfall of ending sentences with a repetitive rising inflection, making it sound as if you are asking a question or making a list.

☐ Lower the vocal pitch (not the volume) when ending sentences to sound confident and conclusive.

☐ Avoid excessive use of the conjunction "and" to connect your sentences and questions.

☐ Escape monotone delivery by putting emphatic stress on key words to stimulate natural inflection.

☐ Slow down and speak in phrases even more deliberately when discussing complicated issues.

Practicing Aloud

☐ Practice on your feet to coordinate your body, brain, and voice.

☐ Practice aloud to build the muscle memory of your articulators: lips, tongue, jaw.

☐ Rough draft aloud; talk first, write second.

☐ Practice aloud behind the wheel when you are driving in your car.

☐ Don't practice talking to a mirror! Mirrors merely make you more self-conscious.

☐ Practice aloud, alone, a lot!

☐ If you have limited time, always practice the first paragraph aloud several times so you can start strong.

☐ If you have limited time, always practice the last paragraph aloud several times so you can end strong.

Appendix 2

Video Self-Review Checklist

Watch for these elements when you critique yourself on video

Feet & Stance

☐ Is your stance dynamic? Are your feet a comfortable distance apart?

☐ Is your body weight centered so it is evenly balanced over both feet?

☐ Watch to see if you stand still at the beginning.

☐ Are your ankles crossed?

☐ Notice whether your feet are shuffling or shifting. Move only with a purpose, not randomly; move to a new location when moving to a new idea.

☐ Moves of a couple of feet look like nervous fidgeting. Move at least six feet when you move.

☐ Look at your feet. Are they moving more than your arms? Feet tend to move too much when the arms move too little. Think: Let your arms do the walking.

Knees & Hips

☐ Knees should be flexible, not locked, as they are when you are standing in a moving bus or subway.

☐ Your hips should be centered over your feet. Avoid sliding one hip too casually over to one side.

Breath Support

☐ Observe your breathing. Breathe consciously before you stand up to control the adrenaline rush and calm your nerves.

☐ Can you see your lungs expanding and contracting? Breathe deeply from your abdominal area to project your voice and flood your brain with oxygen.

Gestures

☐ Are your hands in a ready position? Hands should be touching at your navel, elbows bent 90 degrees.

☐ Avoid the fig leaf position, reverse fig leaf, hands in your pockets, or fondling your pen.

☐ Gestures should be larger in size and longer in duration in order to look and feel natural.

☐ Natural gestures are smoother rather than jerkier, and slower rather than faster. Think smooth and slow.

☐ When do you begin to gesture? Consciously gesture sooner rather than later. Jump-start gestures immediately.

☐ Do you use the "on the one hand... on the other hand" gesture to trigger your instinct to gesture?

☐ You should fill the zone of gesture: a 2'X5' rectangle, two feet from your waist to your chin, and five feet out to the sides.

☐ Are you gesturing when asking questions by extending the arms with palms up? Give the question with your gesture.

☐ Check to see if you use all four options to give questions: right hand, left hand, both hands, and sometimes, none.

☐ Watch for show gestures. Could your hands be more expressive?

☐ Look for the karate *chop* or double karate chop with your hands sideways for the most emphatic delivery.

☐ If there is a lectern, are you touching it at all? Don't lean on the lectern with locked elbows, shoving your shoulders up toward your ears. Don't slouch on the lectern, placing your forearms on the furniture.

☐ Stand up straight at the lectern.

☐ Observe whether you drop your arms to your sides—the *release* position—as you finish a thought. Be your own exclamation mark!

Posture

☐ Look at your body's alignment. Good posture is not shoulders back and chest out! That increases tension.

☐ Good posture is a direction—upward—not a position that is held like a statue.

☐ Your head belongs over your torso (don't lift your chin), not out front in a "chicken neck" position.

☐ Imagine your head is being pulled upward by a bungee cord attached to the top of your skull.

Face

☐ Is your face alive? Adopt your natural face of "introduction," the one you use when you shake hands introducing yourself.

☐ Beware the deadpan "cadaver face." Try parting your lips slightly. Breathe through your mouth and nose.

☐ Notice whether your face and gestures are working together. Natural gestures tend to bring natural animation to your facial expressions. Don't freeze up! Keep gesturing.

Eyes

☐ Are you looking at your listeners? Did you focus on the jury or the witness before you began speaking?

☐ Your should look at the four corners of the perimeter of your jury to define the target area.

☐ Understand your "thinking mannerism": When considering what to say next, do you look up, down, or sideways? Don't look away from people for too long.

☐ Focus your eyes to focus your brain.

Thinking

☐ Don't read to them! *Talk* to them. Which are you doing?

☐ Are there pauses in your delivery? Silence is golden. Silence is your friend. Adrenaline's time warp makes pauses seem inordinately long.

☐ Have you given yourself and your jury time to think?

☐ Time your pauses. How many seconds pass during each one? One second? Two?

☐ Where are you looking? Don't start by looking at and reading from your notes. Focus on the people you are addressing.

☐ You should use your notes like a parachute; go to them if you are about to crash and burn.

☐ Are your notes easy to read? Construct your notes as a visual aid for yourself: write big and keep it simple.

☐ Check to see whether you have defaulted to "serious" or "hostile." Actively choose your attitude. Attitude is a tactical choice.

Speaking

☐ You should hear yourself speak in phrases, not whole sentences. As you begin, use the pace of the *Pledge of Allegiance.*

☐ Listen to your pace. Start slowly by speaking in phrases, then speed up as you get comfortable.

☐ A slow pace signals the importance of what you are saying. Preliminary information may be faster. Persuasive points should be slower.

☐ Have you varied your pace? Sometimes, separate... every... word to achieve a super-slow pace for extra emphasis. Use this technique when you quote documents, witnesses, evidence.

☐ Speaking too softly? Use more breath support.

☐ Is your voice trailing off? Emphasize the final word or phrase in questions.

☐ Beware of the questioning uptick of inflection at the ends of sentences ↘↗. It makes you sound uncertain ↘↗.

☐ Do you drop the pitch of your voice to end sentences conclusively? Think of how newscasters sign off at the end of a broadcast. Listen to hear whether you walk down the steps.

The Law of Opposites

☐ Have you applied the Law of Opposites? For a sentence or even just a phrase, have you done the opposite of what your instinct most often leads you to do?

☐ Listen carefully to hear whether you go slower than your usual pace for emphasis, or speak softer than your usual volume for emphasis.

☐ Watch to see whether you are ever still, rather than animated.

☐ Listen for contrast. Do you ever use longer silences to let the fact finder think?

☐ Notice whether the "s" words could apply to your performance: slower, softer, stiller, and silence.

Bibliography

Amberry, Tom, & Reed, Philip; *Free Throw: 7 Steps to Success at the Free Throw Line*; Harper Collins, New York, 1996.

Burns, Ken; *The Civil War*; television series; Public Broadcasting Service, Washington, D.C., 1989.

Gawande, Atul; *Complications: A Surgeon's Notes on an Imperfect Science*; Picador, New York, 2002.

Goldin-Meadow, Susan; *Illuminating Mental Representations Through Speech and Gesture;* Psychological Science, Vol. 10, No. 4; Washington, D.C., July 1999.

Goldin-Meadow, Susan; *Hearing Gesture: How Our Hands Help Us Think*; Belknap Press, Cambridge, Massachusetts, 2003.

Holzer, Harold; *Lincoln at Cooper Union: The Speech that Made Abraham Lincoln President*; Simon & Schuster, New York, 2004.

Iverson, Jana; *Gesture When There is No Visual Model*, New Directions for Child Development, No. 79; Jossey-Bass, San Francisco, Spring 1998.

Kendon, Adam, ed.; *Gesture and Understanding in Social Interaction*, Research on Language and Social Interaction, Vol. 27, No. 3, special edition; Erlbaum Associates, Hillsdale, New Jersey, 1994.

Kendon, Adam; *An Agenda for Gesture Studies*, Semiotic Review of Books; http://www.univie.ac.at/Wissenschaftstheorie/srb/srb/gesture.html, Thunder Bay, Ontario, Canada, 2001.

McNeill, David; *Hand and Mind: What Gestures Reveal About Thought*; University of Chicago Press, Chicago, 1992.

Ornstein, Robert E.; *On the Experience of Time*; Penguin, New York, 1997.

Stattkus, Dietmar; *Help! I'm Sweating! Causes, Phenomena, Therapies*; Hidrex, Biomedizinische Technik, Wuppertal, Germany, 2006.

Williams, Ted, and Underwood, John; *The Science of Hitting;* Fireside, Simon & Schuster, New York, 1986.

Wilson, Frank R.; *The Hand: How Its Use Shapes the Brain, Language, and Human Culture;* Pantheon Books, New York, 1998.

Index

About the Authors

Brian K. Johnson has worked as a courtroom communication consultant since 1979. Every year he works one-on-one with more than 1,000 attorneys to help them analyze and improve their courtroom communication skills. In addition to teaching advocacy and persuasion to trial lawyers, he also teaches public speaking skills to corporate attorneys. In 2000, he was awarded the Prentice Marshall Faculty Award from the National Institute for Trial Advocacy, the first time in its history this award was given to a communication consultant.

Marsha Hunter is a specialist in training attorneys how to speak persuasively and spontaneously. She is a partner in Johnson and Hunter, Inc., with legal clients throughout the United States, Canada, and in Europe. She teaches communication skills for the National Institute for Trial Advocacy, the Department of Justice, and elite law firms. Marsha Hunter attended The Curtis Institute of Music in Philadelphia, and holds degrees from Embry-Riddle Aeronautical University in Daytona Beach, Florida (Master's of Aeronautical Science) and Arizona State University (Bachelor's of Music).